A HANDBOOK ON THE
PRINCIPLES OF CHURCH BUILDING
FURNISHING EQUIPMENT AND DECORATION

ESME GORDON

PUBLISHED BY THE CHURCH OF SCOTLAND
ADVISORY COMMITTEE ON ARTISTIC QUESTIONS
121 GEORGE STREET, EDINBURGH 2

PRINTED IN GREAT BRITAIN BY

WILLIAM BLACKWOOD & SONS LTD.

A HANDBOOK ON THE
PRINCIPLES OF CHURCH BUILDING
FURNISHING EQUIPMENT AND DECORATION

CONTENTS

PREFACE

In preparing this work for publication, at the invitation of the Church of Scotland Advisory Committee on Artistic Questions, I have received encouragement and help from many which I acknowledge with gratitude. It is to my friend William McCrea that I owe my first and greatest debt: he read the draft and, based on his knowledge and love for his Church coupled with long experiences both as an architect and organist, he gave me fruitful suggestions and made corrections, as all who know him would expect, in the kindest possible way. The Rev. George Paterson, secretary to my sponsors, has also been ungrudging in his careful attention. His searching perusal of my text led to an invaluable series of copious, penetrating and constructive observations on which I have freely drawn. The administrative work in connection with the preparation of my text and the multifarious details associated with publication have also been a secretarial responsibility. Dr Stanley Cursiter, with his ever alert mind, has assisted with clarification of thought and phrase.

The section *Organs and Choirs* has been in part founded on papers made available to me which were prepared for the Church of Scotland by Herrick Bunney and Stuart Harris. By the use of quotation and paraphrase my work was not only made easier but also has in consequence gained much in strength and authority.

When my final draft was nearing completion I met, after an interval of several years, Professor Theodore Sizer, Dean of Cornell University. He then informed me that he had assisted Jonathan Sherman, Suffragan Bishop of Long Island, and his Committee in the preparation of a parallel publication. Through their generosity a copy of *Church Buildings and Furnishings* (The Seabury Press, Greenwich, Connecticut, 1958) was sent to me.

Written from the orientation of a Sister Church I found not only confirmation but much that was relevant to my task.

The great interest that two of my friends have shown I value highly. I have to thank the Very Rev. Dr Charles L. Warr who read my earliest draft and gave me advice founded on his very deep knowledge of the ways of our Church. Dr Ronald Selby Wright scrutinised the completed text and, from his " unbiased reading of history ", has assisted in historical references. He has also contributed largely to the Bibliography which adds so much to this publication as a work of reference. I am all too conscious that these pages can treat their subject matter in a most cursory fashion: all those who seek more authoritative and developed treatment will find the works listed comprehensive and reliable.

I wish to record a word of explanation to those craftsmen and tradesmen who give the Church devoted service when, through their skill, they translate Ideas into Reality. It is repeatedly advised in the ensuing pages that professional opinion should first be sought; this is nothing other than a disinterested recommendation as to how the best results are to be achieved. It is no reflection on those many firms which either execute work or supply materials. God's House demands of us all only the best, and the will, effort, understanding and mutual appreciation of us all are necessary if we are to achieve this end. My own debts in this connection are many, and in gratitude I dedicate this little work to all those who work together in this spirit.

August 1963.   E. G.

INTRODUCTION

THIS handbook has been prepared to guide and inform ministers and kirk sessions who, along with their congregations, are responsible for the communal activities and religious instruction within their parishes. On them also is laid the charge of the buildings both old and new in the great and national traditions of the Church of Scotland. The effectiveness of the life and teaching is dependent on the physical environment. It is hoped that this publication can provide information and stimulation where there are improvements under consideration or problems to solve. It is also thought that some of the advice and guidance may serve those who are called upon to design churches.

The origins of the present work lie in the "Principles of Church Design" which was published shortly after the war by the Church of Scotland Advisory Committee on Artistic Questions under the convenership of the late Rev. Dr J. Arnott Hamilton. He, the chairman and chief author of that book, is remembered with affection by all those who worked with him in all those matters which were so dear to him. When the text of his book was scrutinised in consultation with him with a view to republication it was then felt that there was room for a more extended work embodying greater guidance and factual information. Out of great respect to the memory of Dr Hamilton certain passages from the earlier publication that lay so close to his heart have been re-used and are incorporated into the present text.

It cannot be too strongly emphasised that in setting out the facts contained in this book the Advisory Committee on Artistic Questions does not in any way desire to hamper the initiative of the architect or artist by recommending the rigid or the stereotyped. The Committee is set against imposing limitation on creative genius: it is the intention to encourage originality and individuality to the very utmost limits. While it would have been seductively easy to have included a wealth of illustrations—and plans—to exemplify from the many fine buildings which have arisen in recent years this temptation has been resisted, partly on account of economy, partly to avoid " dating ", but more particularly because the Committee is determined to maintain an open mind. To choose for illustration could be interpreted as to favour.

Many problems that arise are touched on in this work, but no solutions are offered—for every situation must be considered on its own merits. The plea is for a re-examination and a fresh approach to all matters associated with our buildings in the light of the practical demands of to-day; and this must be furthered, by knowledge and intelligent application, towards a solution of true quality in terms of the essential elements of the traditions of the Reformed Church.

General principles there must be for every matter, though they should be of such a nature, and stated as such, that full scope is afforded for the individual solution. The limitations which the Committee suggest should in no sense cramp creative power; the principles are of a broad nature, allowing full play for personal inspiration. These principles if applied practically in the realm of architecture and design would be in keeping with the doctrinal, homiletic and liturgical attitude of the contemporary Church of Scotland. In saying this a guard must be made against the merely fashionable than which nothing dates more rapidly. We seek verities which are eternal: sincerity and integrity are important components. Experiment and courage are sought so that the consequences can be rewarded with a successful crowning. Failures also will occur—even the failure of negative results that arises through any tendency to play safe. This calculated risk is appreciated, for should we be so timid that we venture little, triumph will elude us completely.

The Church of Scotland has its standpoint and its beliefs: its buildings in plan, arrangement and design must be appropriate to, and expressive of, the beliefs and practices. It will be seen section by section in this work how the arrangements of the Church reflect its beliefs—its belief in the public administration of Baptism as entrance into the visible Church of Christ, its belief in the Sacrament of the Lord's Supper as the Sacred Feast where all the faithful gather around the Table to enter into communion with the present Lord, and its belief in the proclamation of the Word as a great means of grace.

It is the wish of the Committee on Artistic Questions to help as many churches as possible. Even the most unpromising church can with thought be changed into a place of beauty. By some wise re-arrangement, by some better furnishings, by an improved scheme of decoration, apparently intractable interiors have been made attractive to a degree beyond expectation. If competent advice be followed the results can be most rewarding.

If any considerable change in an old church is contemplated the greatest care must be exercised. The architect of a former generation has planned his church around interior arrangements: a drastic renovation may bring into being an interior treatment quite inappropriate to the general structure. For example, while the removal of unwanted galleries may greatly improve the appearance of one church, it can make another merely vacant, dreary and difficult for hearing.

To have significance the church must be a source of inspiration and peace to its members and visitors. With beauty its influence is impalpable but sure. Mysteriously, but profoundly, it brings its power to bear upon the human soul. The passage of light across the colour of a wall, the majestic curve of an arch and vault, the radiance of a stained-glass window, the quiet lines of mouldings or a semi-dome of a simple apse may, often in a manner that is unrealised, touch the heart and aid the worshipper profoundly in his approach to God.

It is of course obvious that everyone is not sensitive in the same degree to form and colour. But through their vision the susceptibilities of a greater number of people than is sometimes realised are touched by the beauty of their church. Many simple church-going members who make no claims to critical understanding will speak of the loveliness of their church. They might be unable to express or explain their pride and admiration in detail, but appreciation is present in their minds, and their broad judgment is often wise, sound and true. Enriched even by familiarity and experience, this response may, under the pressure of place, circumstance and time, show itself in differing ways. It may be the ambience of quiet peace which is the joy, or it may lie in the reverential awe which bows the soul before the majesty of God. Whatever may be the manner in which the church building re-acts upon the mind, the admiration for the beauty of the sanctuary can fuse with the quest for truth; in this manner the desire for goodness creates that blessed state which lifts the human soul into the presence of the Eternal.

It is not only because of its effect on men and women that the House of God should be made lovely. Surely with reverence it may be said that it is His will. The glory of God is revealed in the visible creation, in the mountains and the streams, in the forests and the valleys, in the oceans and the plains. By their form and their colour, by their distance and their texture, by the very atmosphere in which they are enveloped, by the light which gleams upon them and the shadows which they cast, on these are suffused with the mysterious element of beauty, a revelation of the transcendent in the material world, a sacramental manifestation of the Most High. The Creator of beauty in the natural order has endowed man with the faculties not only to see and love His handiwork but also has given him the power to make, devise and distinguish that which is made beautiful by the labour of hand and mind. Man can erect those buildings which by proportion, character and nobility impress or elevate: where there is reception he can be inspired to fresh creations in stone, glass or canvas which are a fountainhead of joy to all.

THE CHURCH OF SCOTLAND ADVISORY COMMITTEE ON ARTISTIC QUESTIONS

As the sponsor of this publication it is appropriate at the outset that the form, purpose and scope of the Church of Scotland Advisory Committee on Artistic Questions should be outlined.

The General Assembly of the Church of Scotland, in 1935, approved the proposal of the Reverend Millar Patrick, D.D., to establish the Advisory Committee on Artistic Questions. Dr Millar Patrick was appointed its first Convener and Sir D. Y. Cameron, R.A., R.S.A., its first Vice-Convener. In pursuance of its remit from succeeding General Assemblies this Committee has dealt with many hundreds of requests for advice on church fabrics and furnishings. In recent years the General Assembly has granted permission for the Committee to issue literature dealing with its subject. In 1959 the General Assembly enlarged the membership and reconstituted the strengthened body as one of its standing Committees.

When approached, the purpose of this Committee is to assist to the best of its ability with advice that is primarily of an aesthetic nature. That any such guidance in all probability must be based on severely practical considerations is accepted as essential. Nothing is too large or too small for equally serious attention, and submissions to the Committee range from matters as widely divergent as a colour scheme for a church interior to examination of a stained glass window cartoon or the design for a Communion Chalice.

The Committee is approached through its Secretary at 121 George Street, Edinburgh, to whom the query along with the fullest possible particulars, including relevant photographs, sketches and rough plans to elucidate the problem as fully as possible should be sent.

The membership of the Committee, which works on a purely voluntary basis, can be defined as being " interested " ministers and elders, along with architects and artists.

As most of the matters which come before the Committee demand first-hand knowledge of the church in question, a visit by a deputation is frequently arranged. It will listen, discuss—but not give an opinion. To cover most of Scotland adequately in this fashion the Committee maintains a system of local panels. Following the visit a report is submitted by the deputation, whenever possible in person, to the parent Committee which, having analysed and considered all aspects of the problem, agrees and issues a consolidated Report to the enquirer. For matters of exceptional importance the Committee may be prepared to receive a representative or deputation from the church for joint discussion. On occasions tolerance regarding timing may be needed. The Committee members devote many hours of their time to this work for no reward other than the privilege of assisting. Should the requests come, therefore, in holiday periods or when those most suited are engaged elsewhere, there will be inevitable delay. But every effort is made to act expeditiously: it assists with arrangements when requests are made well in advance.

The accusation has been levelled at this Committee that it cuts across professional interests and livings. This is most seriously refuted. The Committee is prepared to help to the utmost those who want to help themselves. But where there is the slightest element of doubt, or any call for continuous or more searching expert advice, the sum and substance of the Report is invariably that professional guidance be sought.

Being issued by an Advisory Committee there is no compulsion attached to the Reports. But recipients can rest assured that the recommendations represent the best advice that this Committee, with its call on expert and knowledgeable minds, can formulate.

AUTHORISATION

BEFORE it is put in hand, projected work of a permanent nature to church property must have the approval of the responsible authorities. It is well that the nature of the necessary applications be understood, for they embrace all projects ranging from the introduction of either new furnishings, stained glass windows or memorials, to structural alterations or an entirely new building.

Where there is the addition of any new element or internal re-arrangement that is concerned with either furnishing, or commemorative memorial, formal application must be made, with fully explanatory drawings, to the presbytery in which the church is situated. In the majority of cases the request is then forwarded to the General Trustees, on receipt of whose agreement the proposed work can be put in hand.

(It may be observed that there are isolated exceptions to this general rule but these are so rare that for the present purposes they may be ignored.)

Where structural work is concerned, in addition to the foregoing, all cases without exception require the sanction of the local authorities, either municipal or county as may be applicable. Full working drawings, indicating materials, must be lodged along with the appropriately completed form in the manner specified by the authority. For new buildings it may be helpful at an earlier stage to consult the local Fire Officer regarding the planning and construction of escape routes.

For all new buildings and when the project has any outward considerations, e.g., any additions, alterations to external doors or windows, further drawings and completed forms must be lodged so that the local Planning Authority can also give the necessary approval.

CHURCH BUILDINGS TO-DAY

In the past men have dedicated their skill, love and wealth on their churches knowing now in humility, now in pride that their best alone can be barely adequate for this great purpose. As century has succeeded century each branch of the Church has taken the changing dictates of its liturgy and its ritual as the basis of inspiration for creation. These expressions were assimilated, and, having become the platform for greater endeavour, have stimulated further thought and creation. The history of building demonstrates that Man's ability to enclose space has made possible that which we do, and not the converse.

Antiquarianism in Architecture is of recent origin, being consequent on the Napoleonic wars and the Industrial Revolution. Prior to that period it was the tradition to be and build as a modern; thereafter it became modern to be and build as a traditionalist. This attitude is now happily being reversed—but for many of the wrong reasons.

Anyone who ventures an opinion on church building of to-day may go far astray without knowledge of architectural history. In order to understand fully and learn the lessons of our monuments, the purposes that went into their creation must be appreciated. It will then become clear that the triumphs—for triumphs they are—are of interpretation not doctrine. Geology, geography associated with climate, and engineering ability each in its own way has its effect; it is only to be expected that appearances have differed from place to place and from generation to generation. Herein lies the key to " style ", a convenient term which does little more than facilitate the grouping of architectural history into its chapters. At times change has been slow, tempered only by the gradual evolution of knowledge. On other occasions a sudden advance can be initiated by reasons as dissimilar as the introduction of the pendentive and vaulting or the Reformation and the Jesuitical reaction. As long as Church and Society maintain vitality development must continue; the alternative can only be stagnation.

We live in an age of transition and men find analogies with earlier and similar periods. We of to-day seek and see parallels in the more formative times rather than in full-flowering ages. Ever interested in man's activities the thoughtful onlooker also knows that the present cults of violence and of novelty are little more than phases in the pageant of ever-changing fashion. To find eternal verities it is necessary to search more deeply. There must be a warning in all matters against so called " good taste " alone. Uninformed by adequate knowledge and training, taste may be the greatest danger, be backward looking with its roots in mere convention. By reducing all to a level of comfortable security, taste can drain off everything that is of positive character.

Study of the Past can teach much. It must be remembered that our thought, vision and reaction are highly influenced by the passage of time; it is impossible for us either to *see* as the originators saw, or to *feel* as they felt. It nevertheless remains true that should the work be based on sincerity and conviction the ring of truth can be heard resounding directly across the centuries. Hard to destroy completely, it is these qualities alone which bring life to the work of men's hands and makes it sublime.

There is not necessarily any connection between these attributes and size, site, age or expenditure: this is not to say that these last-named attributes cannot and do not have their great effects. And possibly superfluous to mention, whatever may be the dictate of the moment, the essential vitality has neither the remotest connection with the copy nor with any one style as opposed to another. Essential quality also has no connection with that energy which is the violence of reaction. Work born of this conception does not endure: all too soon it is merely old-fashioned. A characteristic of to-day is that whereas

B

society was formerly dominated by an omnipotent church or a cultured aristocracy we have yet to find an equivalent source of intellectual stimulus and demand. The impersonality and compromise of a well-intentioned committee is no alternative to the traditional patron.

In the building of a church success requires fundamental thought which cannot be dissociated from contemporary life. Examination of any of the great monuments handed down to us, revealing the magnitude of the intellectual achievement, has, or should have, a sobering effect. Implicit in our admiration is the recognition that these buildings not only look magnificent but also that they *worked* supremely well. It is our responsibility to find an equally satisfactory theological and aesthetically functional solution to our problems. In whatever light we regard matters we know that ours is not an age of great Faith—humbled as we are by the work of our forefathers, we must find the key to unlock their secret. While this in itself need not be troublesome, to-day's way of thought makes the opening none too easy.

While the Sublime is achieved through conscious intellectual concentration, the Past shows in addition that the mind of the skilled craftsman or unlettered artisan, with complete harmony between intention, material and tool, could and did succeed. This could only have occurred in a comprehensive intellectual climate and cannot be repeated in a machine driven civilisation. The sole assurance for a great tradition of noble building lies in the synthesis of life of an entire people. This is what we seek. Therein is found the stimulus of cross fertilisation; vital and broadly based minds have full and unrestrained opportunity to create, as God meant them to create. With opportunity men have always arisen gloriously to meet the call; as they receive governments, so countries have the architecture they deserve.

Our present civilisation, with all its great material achievements, has its own characteristics amongst which a life-embracing environment is not present: the emphasis has swung from the discipline of the Humanities in such a way that the unity of life is unbalanced. In our churches this makes itself evident with the absence of the outward expression of full and complete life, lived with joy. While it is all the more difficult with our Church buildings for us to achieve the living qualities that tradition expressed with such assurance. virility demands the effort. As we sense and reverence that of our forebears, it is in to-day's monuments that our successors will seek to find our expression of the Good.

While much can be learned, obsessions with the old will obstruct rather than assist. We must comprehend our traditions, look forward to the future courageously and act honestly in terms of to-day. Our Church has suffered and continues to suffer from the self-imposed wounds of sentimentality. We must assimilate contemporary techniques and use them to create a renewed Faith that is flooded with the light of Reality. While the sources, far and near, from which inspiration can be drawn are many, any derivation must be recreated, made Scottish, indigenous and so expressive of our purposes and a true manifestation of our Faith.

On the tenet that form follows function, the quality we seek is inspired common sense, moulded to the requirements of our traditional Faith.

The gist of the matter of the reformed auditory Church is not new. It was written 250 years ago.

" The Capacity and Dimensions of the new Churches may be determined by a Calculation. But still, in our reformed Religion, it should seem vain to make a *Parish-church* larger than that all who are present can both hear and see. The *Romanists*, indeed, may build larger Churches, it is enough if they hear the Murmur of the Mass, and see the Elevation of the Host, but ours are to be fitted for Auditories. I can hardly think it practicable to make a single Room so capacious, with Pews and Galleries, as to hold above 2,000 Persons, and all to hear the Service, and both to hear distinctly, and see the Preacher. In this Church I mention, though very broad, the middle Nave arched up, yet as there are no Walls of a second Order, nor Lanterns, nor Buttresses, but the whole Roof rests upon the Pillars, as do also the Galleries; I think it may be found beautiful and convenient, and as such, the cheapest of any Form I could invent.

" Concerning the placing of the Pulpit, I shall observe—A moderate Voice may be heard 50 feet distant before the Preacher, 30 Feet on each Side, and 20 behind the Pulpit, and not this, unless the Pronunciation be distinct and equal, without losing the Voice at the Last Word of the Sentence, which is commonly emphatical, and if obscured spoils the whole Sense. A *French* Man is heard further than an *English* Preacher, because he raises his Voice, and not sinks his last Words: I mention this as an insufferable Fault in the Pronunciation of some of our otherwise excellent Preachers; which Schoolmasters might correct in the young, as a vicious Pronunciation, and not as the *Roman* Orators spoke: For the principal Verb is in Latin usually the last Word; and if that be lost, what becomes of the Sentence?

" By what I have said, it may be thought reasonable, that the new Church should be at least 60 Feet broad, and 90 Feet long, besides a Chancel at one End, and the Belfrey and Portico at the other. These Proportions may be varied; but to build more room than that every Person may conveniently hear and see, is to create Noise and Confusion. A Church should not be so fill'd with Pews, but that the poor may have room enough to stand and sit in the Alleys, for to them equally is the Gospel preached."

From a letter written by Sir Christopher Wren these words are illuminating and relevant to us to-day. With all admiration for his work it is appreciated that his masterly buildings were first and foremost realistic and simple solutions to complex practical problems.

Those congregations who have inherited a noble church

built by their forefathers are fortunate. Let such peoples remember that it is their privilege to be the trustees for their day and age. They fail in their responsibilities should they either neglect opportunity or omit to ensure that they hand their charge to their successors in good shape and order.

While due care must be taken to see that no feature of historic significance is destroyed or maimed in the interests of so-called "improvements", mere sentiment alone must not obscure. On occasions restraint may be essential to ensure that a requirement or wish of our day—which may be no more than a whim—is not allowed to obliterate something of value. Where there is to be change, there must also be certainty that the new is better than that which it replaces. Should there be the slightest doubt, there must be no hesitation in calling on the best possible professional advice.

There is the church that is neither rich in historical association nor an architectural monument. So familiar can such a building become that its users may be unaware that it is gloomy and even highly inconvenient. It may be painted that indestructable brown, than which nothing is more depressing. It will however be endowed with one essential which outweighs all others; it will be beloved. To such a congregation Opportunity comes and duty is shirked should the church not be made more lovely and expressive of its purpose. It is hard enough to-day to bring the people into the church: to offer dreariness as the setting for Divine Worship is one means of making certain that the necessary partnership of a very vital younger generation will be lost. Here again the caution must be repeated. Where there is the very slightest doubt, knowledgeable opinion should be sought before even minor alterations to work of any age are undertaken. For—all too easily—a fine canopied pulpit can be destroyed or a simple little country church, possibly a perfect example of the traditional setting for our worship, can be ruined in innocent endeavours at "improvement". The caveat refers also to Victorian work: there are fine interiors of dark mahogany, gleaming brass and glass gas or oil light fittings, the loss of which would be regrettable.

To those who take part in the building of a church is the great experience and responsibility of creating a new environment, for they can express Faith in terms of to-day. In every probability this will be for the community of a re-housing scheme. To such the Golden Rule is to discard any stylistic prejudice, for church design must be approached from its fundamentals. The poor buildings that we see are frequently the consequence of the absence of knowledge, not money. The realities of requirements should kill any lurking sentimentality and flood with light the significance of good design.

At this point it is well to consider the meaning of " church ", that little group of buildings planned as an entity and erected to serve every aspect of the religious life of the parish. There is no connection whatsoever between the barren voids that dishonour the name, and the House of God which is reverently spiritual in form and content. This work is a reiteration of a heart-felt plea that our churches in their simplicity shun niggardliness and that nakedness which is nothing other than a misunderstood and misplaced form of obsolete puritanism.

To achieve a masterly solution (and none other is worth having) there must be an agreed initial statement of requirements. This should be followed by the appointment of an architect who must be selected with care. The architect uses his client as a mind on which he can work, for, as with all creative processes, conception follows fertilisation. It is for this reason that whenever possible there should be an embryonic congregation led by its minister rather than a distant committee with no direct and long-term interest in the project. The relationship between client and architect, seldom easy, must be one of complete mutual trust and understanding. The minister must be strong and lead his committee which should be small in numbers and liberally minded. Experience shows that large committees, being unwieldy and impersonal, tend to ensure compromise results which satisfy neither promoters nor authors. With the architect any and all questions should be discussed; this should lead to fuller developments, for the architect, an unconscious teacher, will have his own contributions to make. To achieve maturity encouragement must be given to change during the formative period (which is to say up to the approval of final sketch designs) but thereafter the desire to make alterations must be resisted. If not, the consequences, affecting unforeseen aspects of the building, lead to loss of unity, increased costs and mutual recriminations with all their bitterness. A successful building is a monument to a happy partnership in which the client not only plays a large part but also carries heavy responsibilities.

Building is expensive, as it always has been. In this connection there are points which should be borne in mind. First, the architect. He costs money, but more than earns it in safeguarding his clients' interests. The better the architect so are increased the possibilities of more distinguished results and fullest returns for expenditure. As all charge fees based on an identical scale there is nothing to prevent an approach to the man ideal for the project. This is not to say that an architect of real vision may not inspire possibilities far beyond those initially intended. He can lead—not mislead—his client to an even greater goal.

Second. An overlarge expenditure is not essential to produce architecture. Indeed limited funds can be a great stimulation to creative design. But enduring and effective as they are, materials of quality are almost invariably dear—but not expensive—and in cases of stringency their introduction should be confined to points of emphasis.

Third. It is a mistake to leave work incomplete. How many key stones have been " left boasted for carver " which will never feel the chisel's edge? With a church, however, it can be both possible and politic to provide merely the basic shell to act as a stimulus to the congregation. Paradoxically, all which pedestrian minds deem unnecessary must be complete, and only absolute essentials left unfinished. In this way an outstanding sanctuary treatment may have to await a generous gift, the final treatment for the windows only becomes possible after the building debt has been paid and stalls and falls become objectives for congregational effort. To avoid chaos, the safeguard is to have a master plan co-ordinating all that is to be incorporated.

Fourth. Stupid so-called economies must be avoided. Churches are built to last and should be fitting charges to hand to our successors. Short-term and often blind attempts to reduce expenditure—an omission here and a change there—can and frequently do lead to the more costly rectification.

Fifth. It must be realised that many cheaper materials demand greater expenditure on recurring maintenance. A forecast should therefore be made of the financial burden that is being created. Before final decisions are taken there should be a rigorous examination of such elements as inferior roofing, walls and woodwork, particularly external, requiring frequent attention. Ventilation and heating must be studied. Unreasonably large areas of glass with increased heat losses and requiring much cleaning can prove an embarrassment to congregational funds.

Sixth. In planning and paying for a church, within all reason provide space—length, breadth and most particularly height. Regardless of the type of plan or the form of the church cramped conditions are intolerable. Of greatest importance of all, this arises in the sanctuary: freedom for dignity and movement are at a complete discount in cramped surroundings. As for the members, they require freedom to circulate, room to pass and (often forgotten) many like to have space to be able to kneel when they say their prayers to the Maker.

Seventh. The plan should envisage and provide, at least in skeleton form, for the future. Potential growth must be envisaged. Those who follow and have to find additional accommodation will be grateful for the ease by which this may be achieved.

Much could be written on the topic of maintenance of churches and church buildings. Throughout these pages consideration for such matters has coloured the text. At the present juncture let it be sufficient that the importance be stressed with a further, and appropriate, quotation from Sir Christopher Wren on unchanging human nature.

"The Church-wardens Care may be defective in speedy mending Drips; they usually white-wash the Church and set up their Names, but neglect to preserve the Roof over their Heads: It must be allowed, that the Roof being more out of Sight, is still more unminded."

On occasions congregations are asked to receive gifts for their church. The presentation may be a memorial window or tablet, communion plate, embroideries or perhaps a new Holy Table or pulpit. To cope with these matters each congregation should have a small standing committee of which the minister must be the key member. This committee should have access to trained aesthetic opinion as the responsibilities can be heavy. It must be realised that as acceptance of any gift implies that it will remain in the church *sine die*, care is necessary. Care must be taken that the work is in itself well designed, care must be taken that the new relates happily with the existing surroundings and care must be taken to avoid the superficial and seductive attractions of the novel. The solution lies in the skill of the artist or craftsman with his individual and purpose-made work being infinitely preferable to the stock articles supplied by commercial Ecclesiastical Furnishers. The work of the sincere artist invariably will increase the urgency of communication. It may be observed that the beliefs of the craftsmen have no relevance. That they may not necessarily coincide with the church's ideas of Faith is of no consequence, for who can question either the varying aspects of conviction or from whence comes talent and the ability to create?

Extreme tact may be needed when devoted members offer their own work. To take a single, if obvious example, no doubt embroideries may be technically of the highest order, but the approach to design can, and frequently does, leave much to be desired. The solution does not lie in the purchase of a mechanically produced transfer.

Arising from the foregoing is the relationship between devotional aid and aesthetic worth. Bad stained glass can be claimed as helpful to worshippers—a moral judgment that could not arise where there is any real grasp of values. Frequently personal likes and dislikes, probably based on ignorance, are expressed: these are of no consequence. However convenient they may be as labels there is no such thing as " period " art or " modern " art—there is only art or its absence and this can almost always be recognised by those whose training and reputation entitles them to their views. To introduce into a church anything that being sham does not proclaim truth in all its aspects is nothing short of heresy. If the intention is to deceive, be it through an imitation organ, or simulated marble, we must remember that, while we in our ignorance may be misled, God hears and sees all.

These paragraphs are intended to convey that all churches are held and administered by their congregation for and on behalf of God in Whom the ultimate ownership is vested. The importance of this statement is enhanced by the dominance of one solitary and crowning fact: the human soul is in an identical relationship. Both must be made as perfect as possible under God's guidance. It must be realised that this attribution of all to the Divine and Eternal Majesty of God will override all earthly commemoration, all our short-lived conceptions of use and habit and all that we do and create in the name of our Church. This is comprehensive. Its embrace runs from each element as small as a new offering bag to additions as dominant as a new window. Each detail must be as nearly perfect as possible for its purpose, every new work added to a church must also add to the environment—all must play their parts in the song of praise so that the whole is greater, by far, than the sum of its parts. And by instruction, a new addition to any Church of Scotland fabric, be it furnishing, memorial or window, must state in some form or shape its dedication and purpose first and foremost—" To the Glory of God ".

Emphasis has been laid on sincerity. But in being truthful it is well to realise that our immediate successors may not agree with our expression, for theirs may be a time of reaction. True, full and general assessment will come thereafter. We are committed to a task, and it shall suffice if we are faithful not to fashion, but to Truth. We like our churches to be inviting and cheerful as we strive to unite in our struggle with the evils of the 20th century world. In time, opinions will change and doubtless, much that we stress to-day, believing that we purify and restore our Faith to its true form, will be discarded. This is encouraging. Any church that remains static and does not temper itself to the spiritual essence and calls of its day withers away. Moreover, as has been noted, it is the living works, the sincere and honest works of the past that we revere and which speak to us. With conviction our work may possibly be similarly regarded by posterity; without, failure will certainly now and hereafter be evident.

ORIENTATION

WHILE the direction of a Reformed Church has no symbolic significance practical considerations frequently have. Other things being equal, there is no reason why the church should not be directed towards the east and thus pay respect to a tradition that runs through the ages. Whatever the orientation may be, it is a convenient custom to relate all that is in a directional church to the sanctuary as being the *liturgical* east end. Before touching on the points relevant to orientation a few remarks regarding the traditions and the liturgical aspects may be of interest.

Orientation to the east had its origins in the days of prehistory; the first glimpse of each dawn was synonymous with the end of the fear of the night's darkness. With their advanced knowledge of astronomy and geometry, Egyptians were able, when they wished, to orientate their buildings. The instinct, now deep rooted, was continued by the Greeks, who habitually built the pronaos of their temples in such a way as to allow the sun's first rays to shine and illuminate the deity identified with the statue enshrined in the cella.

The Byzantines and Early Christians continued the established tradition of an eastward inflection now towards the geographic position of the Holy Land hallowed with new significance. On occasions the direction of the church was reversed so that the officiating priest faced both east and his people across the altar. Throughout medieval Christendom a slight, but new variation was accepted when it was arranged that the great east window let in the first glimpse of the rising sun on the day of the saint to whom the church was dedicated.

Much that is accepted by the Church is Christian by adoption. A simple example is the buttressing effects of nave, chancel and transepts in a cruciform building which provides a convenient peg for symbolism.

To revert to the subject so far as it affects a Presbyterian church, there is nothing to be said that is not essentially practical. Having regard to the placing and planning of the building on its site, the prevailing wind and the position of any trees that can be preserved and for doors both in themselves and relative to carriageways are all important. The very shape and condition of the site should assist in establishing the design. A further important consideration is the sun. Decision must be made as to where the brightest fields of illuminated wall surface and window areas should occur at certain times of the day. The exigencies of the general design may call for heavy texturing or darker glass to lessen the strain of overbrightness. And likewise care should be taken to obviate glare in the eyes of both preacher and congregation. The logic of a reconciliation between such factors may well point the way to an assymetrical solution.

REGARDLESS of race or clime, it is inconceivable that any temple should stand without its altar, the visible link joining the tangible with the intangible. In the case of churches, the bulk of the fabric is in essence the shell that protects and shelters those worshipping in fellowship. But the Communion Table, which for the Church of Scotland has supplanted the altar, remains as the precious symbol that directly associates the living with the Eternal. The sanctuary is that part of the building set apart as the scene and setting for our supreme acts of worship around the Table. At all times in the face of the congregation it must therefore be equal to its purpose. It should be designed with thoughtful reverence, constructed as perfectly as possible and completed to capture the spirit of Eternal Peace and Tranquillity.

It is, of course, desirable to provide seating for those who may be grouped round the Holy Table; this is a reversion to the Early Christian form. In the days of the primitive church, often with the orientation west to east, the presiding bishop occupied an elevated throne behind the altar with his clergy ranging on either side at a lower level around the semi-circle of the apse. In this fashion a celebrant was able to officiate facing both the congregation and the east across the altar. The concept that both clergy and laity should face a liturgical east, resulting in the priest turning his back to his people at certain moments in the service, was of later origin.

The seating to be provided must be sufficient and reasonably widely spaced adequately to accommodate the maximum numbers participating who may on occasions be gowned. There must be room to move—and that with dignity. No cramping which might create embarrassment or awkwardness in passing can be tolerated. Loose cushions for kneeling can be added, each upholstered in a colour that accords with the setting. Backs should be given to all seating for comfort and to protect the walls behind. While such chairs or benches can be quite simple, it will be realised that although frequently not in use they will be seen by the congregation at all times. Indeed they can be looked upon as part of the constant and eloquent symbol of the greatest Mystery of our Faith, and as such must be regarded as a permanent part of the sanctuary furnishing. They are therefore at their best when treated as permanent stalls.

Greater emphasis can be given to any seat that may be required for the officiating clergyman. While such a chair can punctuate and give importance to the centre point, its usefulness remains in question and there should be no place for any article, no matter how lovely, which is purposeless. No minister should be behind his Table save at moments of supreme importance: on such occasions he should not sit. If it is desired that a seat be provided for the minister, it is infinitely preferable that this be placed at the side, fronted by a *prie-Dieu*. In larger churches, the sight lines may well demand that the height of the Table is increased beyond the normal. In these instances consideration for the comfort of the clergyman presiding at a Communion Service may necessitate a step behind the Table; this slight elevation will also give the minister a position of greater dignity and command.

To contribute to the sense that here is the most valued and hallowed portion of the church, the floor of the sanctuary should be " hard ". Stone or marbles can be used with great effect. In these cases a note of additional interest, colour, physical comfort and reduction of clatter can be found by introducing a strip of firmly fixed carpeting, the full width of the Table, leading thence across the sanctuary floor and down any approach steps.

It is characteristic of our interpretation of Divine Service in churches built for this purpose that the people and the Table be brought into the closest possible relationship. From this it can be assumed beyond doubt that a long deep chancel, with the Table at the far end, has no relevance in the Reformed Church. It certainly also means that a Sanctum Sanctorum divided from the laity by a screen is as out of place as is the introduction of the choir occupying chancel seats between the Table and the congregation.

For full achievement of this very desirable link of intimacy with the people, an association which assists in engendering the sense of God's family around His Table, there is a more fundamental possibility which must be examined. The suggestion, which has been used most successfully, is to bring the Holy Table and the essential associated furnishings forward so that they are located in the heart of the congregation. It is on the development of such lines that we of to-day can make our contribution to church planning.

There are alternative possible arrangements, any of which can act as the greatest possible stimulus to the imagination in shaping and forming the building. For undoubtedly the functioning of the church will be reflected in its inward and outward appearance. The objective is, of course, to arrange matters so that the greatest number of people are seated as close as possible to the Table with unobstructed sight lines. The sacred furnishings could be situated on the centre point of a circular or many sided building. Or perhaps the Table could be placed well forward from either a long or short side of a rectangular structure with the congregation grouped around three sides. Yet further alternatives are to locate the sanctuary towards the apex of a triangular or fan-shaped plan, or on the chord of a semi-circle.

In the more traditional circumstances, where the sanctuary occurs in a recessed Chancel, the walls are no place for monuments, tablets or any secular elements such as flags and banners. But the furnishing cannot be looked upon as complete if the sign of our Faith, the Cross, is not in the dominant position.

Acceptable on the face of the Communion Table, it is better to have the Cross larger and more elevated, either fixed to or out from the rear wall, or suspended by visible chains or cords. In considering the design of such a feature, simplicity coupled with perfect proportions must be sought. In solitary impressiveness, the significance must be instantly recognised from all view points. This end should not be defeated by making an over elaborate version of a Celtic Cross which in its elemental form can be appropriate. It is important also to exercise care that the impact is not weakened by the over-frequent introduction of the Cross form. The Cross as a major feature should be restricted to this point alone. In placing the Cross it is well to see that it is located sufficiently high above the floor. While it is regrettable to have the Sign obscured by the standing clergyman, it is all the more so when it appears to grow from his head. It should therefore be carefully positioned so that it is visible in its entirety at all times and, so far as possible, from all seats. The material used must be handled and treated with the utmost respect, choice being dependent on the nature of the surroundings and the effects that are sought. Dark stone, polished hardwood or wrought-iron can be impressive against light walls. Burnished metal or gilded wood pinned out or suspended clear of the wall, possibly with side lighting to cast interesting shadow patterns, can similarly be used with fine results. Variations of these treatments take their places against a sombre background or textile. Effect can be heightened on occasions by forming the edges of the Cross as a slight moulding picked out with a contrasting note of colour which defines and separates the Cross from its background.

A degree of indirect lighting can be effective in giving warmth and magnetism to the sanctuary. However, every effort must be made to avoid the very real peril of the theatrical. Such lighting, picking out the Cross (which under no circumstances must itself be lit) and bathing the area with a gentle

C

flood of illumination must be discreet. One or two electric plug points in convenient but inconspicuous positions should be provided. These have uses ranging from special lighting effects and the Christmas Tree to floor polishers and vacuum cleaners.

There is, of course, no compulsion to have an " east " window. Indeed, if the church is not large and the cill sufficiently high, the sanctuary can be all the better without the glare conditions that the bright field of such windows can create.

At the lower levels the surrounding walls can be finished to provide the essential setting and character for the Communion Table. Good hardwood panelling, stone or polished marble dado treatment, well chosen hangings or mural paintings can each be appropriate. It is most important that design, texture and colour arrangement each be most carefully considered and regulated to give the maximum possible effect. Of all parts of the church it is the sanctuary which is seen by all, at all times and under circumstances which vary from the normal services to Thanksgivings, Communion, Baptisms, Weddings and Funerals. Success is dependent on restraint.

The introduction of flowers into the sanctuary brings a token of God's beauty and fragrance of life into the setting created by Man. Being rightly accepted, there will at best be inconvenience should adequate provision not be made for the presence of the necessary vases or containers. These may be placed either on the floor, on well designed and steady stands on either side of the Table, alternatively they may be set on brackets, corbels or shelves on the side walls, or across the rear: not being sacramental they have no place on the Communion Table itself. On occasions the enthusiastic exuberance of those who " do " the flowers can go over far. The sanctuary is no place for an impressive flower show and it may be necessary to guard against the magnificence of an over-generous display which, elsewhere impressive, in this setting is merely vulgar.

In passing, a note must be made regarding the shape of the

vases themselves. The elegant, trumpet form that appears so suitable in this setting is not necessarily ideal for flower arrangement. Those responsible should be consulted. The general desire at the moment appears to be for deep and wide vases that can easily contain crumpled chicken netting to steady stems and plenty of water. A caution is given elsewhere against brass.

There is the possibility in some churches of a further, if occasional, use for the sanctuary. This is that, being the central, focal point to which all else within the building is directed, this area becomes the scene for major choral and orchestral works or dramatic performances. This can bring the association of this area on the one hand with the choir and organ on the other into a new and unexpected relationship. There is no occasion here to examine the character or nature of the works that might be performed: the intention is not only correct that the church should fully play its part in the lives of its people but also, following a healthy tradition, that religion should in every way foster the best of man's creative work. Plans should therefore be scrutinised, if not prepared, with those possibilities in mind. Is there a sufficiency of free floor space, with reasonable access and egress? And there should also be suitable controls for all lighting in a convenient position. It is also to be remembered that many additional lights inevitably will be installed and that theatrical producers can be careless about overloading circuits. Provision should therefore be made through the inclusion of extra circuits and plug outlet points.

THE COMMUNION TABLE

At the Communion Table is administered that sacrament which was instituted by Our Lord and Saviour " for the perpetual remembrance of the sacrifice of Himself in His death, the sealing all benefits thereof unto true believers, their spiritual nourishment and growth in Him, their further engagement in and to all duties which they owe unto Him, and to be a bond and pledge of their communion with Him, and with each other, as members of His mystical body ". It must not be overlooked that it is the Table which stands at all times in the face of the congregation as the outward symbol of this supreme union. The Table is therefore all important and must be carefully considered both from the point of view of function and appearance.

As the central point of focus in any church, the maximum possible visibility from all parts should be sought. Depending on circumstances the height should be from 3 feet to 3 feet 9 inches. Successful sight lines may entail elevating the Table above the general floor level: steps which can and do give dignity to the setting must be positioned so that they do not inconvenience the movement of elders and clergy during the service. A short flight leading to a platform area, with the Table itself resting perhaps 4 feet back from the top riser on a further single base of one step, is a satisfactory solution. Wherever possible steps should not exceed 5 inches in height with 14 inch treads and it minimises risk if contrasting colours can be used for emphasis. Such steps are preferable with no nosings. The aim should be to have each flight an odd and not an even number of risers, since this makes for the comfort of starting and stopping.

The length and breadth of the Table, which should be as generous as possible, will in part be dictated by the area in which it stands. It should be large enough not only to carry with ease the sacred vessels including all the flagons, but, to receive its due dignity, be relative to the surrounding space. It is important that the top project slightly over the vertical sides both to preserve the characteristics of a table and also to ensure the graceful draping of the white linen cloth used at the time of Communion.

Christian tradition suggests that the top should have engraved on it five small Crosses, symbolic of Christ's wounds. Reverence for the inherent symbolism and the living acts performed at this Table can occasion the seemliness of maintaining—at all times other than when Communion is being celebrated—a longitudinal textile overlay which should hang down well over both ends. Such covers, bringing with them decorative possibilities, can follow the liturgical sequence, red, green, purple, white or gold, that will be echoed in the Pulpit falls.

It is a regrettably common error in the Church of Scotland for the Table to be used to carry trivia. The Table is sacramental and on it should be laid only such articles as are used in the service. This is not only right, but " follows a very old tradition of western Christendom, a tradition of keeping down to a minimum the ornaments, and one which was due to the belief that it was desirable on the grounds of reverence and fitness to have nothing but what was necessary for the celebration of the divine mysteries ". It is logical therefore to place on the Table, in addition to the Communion cups and plates, a small lectern or cushion, perhaps the alms dishes and any thing which may be brought for dedication. The Table, it is recommended, should not carry flower vases which should be restricted to brackets either behind or at the sides. They can also be placed on the floor flanking either end of the Table.

It is best, naturally, if the Table can be permanently located to give the minister all the space he requires to officiate and kneel. But in difficult surroundings it can be accepted that, to improve sight lines for Communion, the Table may be brought forward, thereby also creating greater surrounding space for minister and elders. When not moved forward in this way such a Table can normally remain close to a rear wall, which it must not touch.

Being neither altar nor tomb, our Table must not assume their characteristics or outward forms. Nor is there any restriction such as is found with an altar regarding proximity to any grave or sepulchral slab. Stone or marble can imply the incorporation of the relic which tends to create a shrine. To make the distinction clear, let our Tables be of fine, living wood.

This is not the place to decree whether Tables be open or closed since either can be appropriate. The earliest Holy Tables in the primitive church were of tall table form, usually on a stout central support, or with four legs (on occasions five, which provided the perfect location for the Crosses that were engraved on the top). Should the latter examples be used it will be observed that as the congregation can *see* through, seemliness may suggest that some form of screen may be necessary.

Being the very heart of the church, the Communion Table should be as perfect as possible. This does not imply extravagance, for many a lovely article has been made using deal, paint—and brains. However, the Table frequently provides a field for craftsmanship which may be in relief or inlay. The restrained use of gold (let it be burnished leaf and not metallic paint) and colour, enhancing appearance, can help to accentuate design and modelling. The combination, splendidly heraldic, of gold and vermilion, which was so commonly employed in medieval woodwork, is effective.

Ornamentation must not be trite. It is all too easy to fill spaces with arches, quatrefoils and other devices but in so doing there is risk of achieving the stereotyped or commonplace. If used, such forms should frame and enclose or incorporate symbols, the choice of which can be made from the many appropriate to the Holy Table in a Christian church. Lettering, of course, may be introduced but only subject to certain limitations; it must be legible to avoid defeating its purpose. There is nothing sacrosanct about the all too familiar Gothic forms which are merely difficult to read. The wording must be worthy of the position. It is undesirable that any record of a gift or bequest should appear on the front. Such matters, which are of course most important, should be confined inconspicuously to the back or possibly a side.

One of the shortcomings of architectural design to-day is that shaping and profiling to stir the desire to touch and caress tend to be forgotten. The Table should exemplify par excellence this tactile quality. This characteristic must be reconciled with carrying power, for the Table must convey its character and message to the farthest seat.

Reference must be made to a lovely Scottish tradition which remains alive here and there. This is to have the congregation join in the Communion service at the very Table itself and not merely in its presence. This very personal and intimate interpretation is not more generally used because of the time occupied in administering the elements in this manner to a large congregation. This happy custom should not be idly neglected or discarded; perhaps its use could be more widely introduced with gain in devotion and individuality.

The practical points of importance that must be considered are, first: as the congregation will move (possibily in relays) there must be room to circulate freely. Second: as the communicants will be seated at the Table, it should be of a suitable height (say 2 feet 6 inches to 2 feet 8 inches). And third—and most important—while additional tables may be added to extend seating capacity, the Communion Table always present, which can be designed as " extending ", will continue to be used.

THE PULPIT

From the pulpit the preacher proclaims and interprets the Word of God to the congregation which is gathered together within the church. It is from the pulpit that the message of God's love in Christ is delivered in words which by the grace of God comfort the heart, enlighten the understanding, ennoble the character and sanctify the spirit. The importance of the pulpit cannot be overstressed and its position and form must be carefully studied so that it may be perfectly suited to its function. While there is nothing binding, the general traditional position for the pulpit is on the left-hand side, " north ", of the chancel opening. There is also a well-established reformed tradition for the centre pulpit, particularly in the Scottish T-plan churches.

It is necessary at the outset to accept the real and dual nature of Presbyterian worship—the Word and the Sacrament—and relate the one to the other in the layout and furnishing. If it can be accepted that the Communion Table must be placed in a position of dominance, then the pulpit can be located either centrally, to one side behind or brought forward to one side of the chancel opening. There are exceptional occasions, particularly with long naves, when it is sensible to accept a reversion to a medieval practice, normal when there was an enclosed choir. This is to place the pulpit to one side (traditionally the north) of the congregation in the nave, perhaps one-third of the distance westwards. The correct position for the pulpit is, therefore, that which can be accepted both liturgically—which is simple—and architecturally—which may be more difficult—and from which the preacher can best be heard. As most ministers find the delivery of the sermon a period of strain, everything possible should be done to lessen this undesirable condition. It assists if the preacher is of and amongst his people and not isolated by having the Communion Table and all its free floor space between him and the front rows of seating. This suggests that for to-day, without being dogmatic, the "forward side" pulpit, leaving the Holy Table in dignified and splendid isolation, is to be preferred. The pulpit should certainly be placed so that all—or at least the majority—of the congregation can also see it. With the association between hearing and seeing, the invisible preacher can expect attention to wander from his sermon to the study of windows, wall tablets and new hats.

The foregoing remarks are made with every respect and regard to the many existing Scottish churches in which the pulpit has been placed against the end wall. Should any re-arrangement or replacement of a central pulpit and other furnishings be contemplated for any reason, most serious consideration is needed. The original architect will have con-ceived his plan with no other placing in view. Even were it possible, drastically to alter this location may destroy symmetry and create more problems than it solves. Should a change be essential it may well be preferable, while adhering to the central position, either to modify the pulpit or have it replaced in the same position.

With all pulpits the treatment of the floor space in front is of importance. It should be left unencumbered and free of all furnishings. A "hard" floor—perhaps stone or marble—will materially assist with acoustics. As most ministers find a low pulpit more comfortable, creating a greater intimacy between preacher and congregation leading to a sympathetic under-standing and ease of approach, a very high one should be avoided. An exception would be when conditions such as galleries that are fully occupied, with difficult sight lines, make height essential. For the average church the floor of the pulpit should be approxi-mately level with the shoulders of the seated congregation. The level will of course be raised as the size of the building increases.

The pulpit must be sufficiently ample to afford the gowned preacher all ease of movement, taking care that nothing is done which can add any unnecessary strain to the delivery of the Gospel message. An internal floor area, which for comfort should be carpeted, of approximately 12 square feet should be regarded as a minimum. A small seat should be incorporated. The cope or top ledge of the pulpit should be some 3 feet 3 inches above its floor. It is important that there should be no space left for " artistic " reason between side and floor, since vision of clerical footwear, polished or unpolished, should be made impossible.

The book board, large enough to take two foolscap sheets side by side, should be adjustable both for height and angle and must be absolutely steady. Some covering for this book board will probably be essential. This can take the form of a pulpit fall or an upholstered cushion with the possibilities of the generous swagger of cords and tassels. Should the latter be of fabric and additional enrichment desirable, here is an excellent field for colour, design and workmanship. All three are of importance. The material—or materials, should the sequence of liturgical colours be accepted—must be of the best quality. If it is to be embroidered or appliqued it must be chosen with this end in view. The design to be worked must be sufficiently bold for it to carry and should avoid the obvious in subject matter. No matter who executed such work, the craftsmanship must not show the all too obvious hand of the amateur.

To avoid the dangerous use of the cope there must also be a shelf for service books, papers and a glass of water. An open topped narrow box into which papers and books can be slid is useful.

While the preacher and his script must be adequately lit, neither must be subjected to glare from either natural or artificial light. The customary book board strip light alone, which floods paper and midriff with brilliance but leaves the speaker's face lost in gloom, is unacceptable. Additional top light is necessary. The switch controlling the pulpit lighting must be neatly positioned but sufficiently conspicuous for the benefit of visiting preachers.

In Scotland and elsewhere many pulpits in the past were furnished with impressive canopies. Such a feature can be added to-day—but only when it is functionally indispensible for acoustic purposes—and offers a splendid opportunity for imaginative design. Nevertheless, subject to the position of the pulpit, restraint may be necessary to make certain that the additional prominence thus given to a pulpit does not bring it into over-severe competition with the sanctuary. To be effective accoustically, as can be proved graphically, the extent of the canopy must be considerably greater than the area of the pulpit. The underside—the reflecting surface—must be "hard" and not absorbent and can be shaped so as to assist in the distribution of reinforcing reflected sound, particularly with reference to distant seating. The smaller canopies merely pander to the sense of the preacher's self-importance.

The means of access to any pulpit is important both functionally and aesthetically. Those hidden steps which give to the approach the sudden and comic effect of a pantomime trap door should be avoided wherever possible. The movements of the minister, both his coming and his going, should be with dignity and in the full sight of the congregation.

A staircase, however simple it may be, offers a splendid opportunity for gracious design. The "going" should be easy —say 6 inch risers with 12 inch treads as the steepest acceptable angle. Should the steps be slippery or noisy they should be carpeted. The width must be generous for the easy passage of the robed preacher and there must be a steady handrail to grip and to guard any open side. Should safety require a little door as part of the side of the pulpit, it should open in to the pulpit and not out over the steps: from this it follows that the free floor area of the pulpit must be large enough to allow for the swing with comfort.

The materials that may be used for the construction of the pulpit are almost limitless; choice will almost inevitably be governed by expenditure and the most appropriate character for the particular setting. From the very simplest little church with white-washed plaster on a brick base and a hardwood cope to the large interior where there is a place for noble woodwork, chiselled stone, or either cast or wrought metal, all can be highly successful if designed with sensitivity and skill. The prospects of success lie in the last sentence: it is not so much what we do, as how we do it that is of consequence. Should the intention be to acquire a distinguished piece of furniture that will occupy an important and conspicuous focal point within the church then it must be designed specially and with the utmost care and thought. This is the means by which creative work is obtained. On the other hand, should the congregation be satisfied with no more than good workmanship, associated with the somewhat thoughtless repetition of older and too often meaningless architectural features at a cost that may be no less than the purpose made, then they should consult the illustrated catalogues of the commercial ecclesiastical furnishers.

THE LECTERN

THE lectern is an article of furniture which, though by no means universal, is familiar in the Church of Scotland at the present day. However different the form may be, the contemporary form in the Scottish Church can be looked upon as the successor of the reader's desk, from which the Scripture lessons were read in the post-Reformation period. The reader's desk occupied a position, often within an enclosed space, immediately below or as a lower part of the pulpit. It is interesting to note from the frequent allusion in post-Reformation ecclesiastical records to " letternes " that the nomenclature remained constant.

Whether or not there should be a lectern in any particular church depends largely upon circumstances. If it be the custom for an assistant minister or a layman to read the Lessons it will be of so great a convenience as to be almost a necessity. When there is no special reader, a minister may sometimes find it useful for the reading of Scripture, while he conducts the rest of the service from the pulpit or elsewhere. Even when not used at ordinary public worship the lectern can often be a useful adjunct from which services of a simpler nature may be conducted for smaller groups. Under these circumstances it might suitably be installed in a little side chapel, where a comparatively small number may gather to join in prayer or attend to the regular exposition on the Bible.

Whatever form the lectern assumes it is always important that the bookrest should be really steady, at such an angle and height and also adequately illuminated so that the Bible can be read with ease; if the top can be made to adjust for height and angle it will be an advantage. The base can well be elevated on one or more steps above the general floor level. Audibility will be assisted if the lectern is backed by a wall—leaving only sufficient room for the movement and comfort of the reader. Being a conspicuous feature with limitless possibilities for treatment, the importance does not require stressing. From the early Christian Church the ambo as a respond to the pulpit reaches us; the design can then be either identical with the pulpit, slightly modified and reduced or completely different. For materials the choice can range from stone and marble through the metals to hardwood or brick plastered and painted.

A traditional design, now possibly outworn, is the eagle with outstretched wings on which the Bible lay. Such lecterns were usually made either of brass or wood, the eagle being used, perhaps, as the symbol of St John the Evangelist and therefore more narrowly associated with the Gospels alone.

Another form which can have the advantage of portability consists of an oak or other hardwood desk, shaft and base of a much simpler nature. This type can range from the unadorned to an elaborate construction providing a wide field for sculptured decoration; it is possible to enrich the face of the desk with carving and to elaborate the supports.

A third type affords much greater scope for the display of craftsmanship. The sloping desk is supported by two " haffits " —side boards or panels—which extend down to the floor. The space between the haffits may be enclosed by a panel which provides a good field for significant ornamentation. The long narrow verticals which are the main feature of this form will be found to be very suitable surfaces for standing figures in bas-relief or for lettering.

For all of these a pair of bookmarks is required for the Bible, which rests upon its desk, to hang over the front of the lectern and fall down at the back. The ends are well suited for emblems, for which there is wide scope, to be embroidered on the material.

The placing of the lectern is not always an easy matter. If the church be one with a central pulpit, no real difficulty presents itself with regard to the position. It can suitably stand at one angle of the chancel area. With the baptismal font at the opposite angle a balance is obtained. The lectern and font should not be in line with the Table but in front, or, if that be undesirable, behind its line. Where the sanctuary is apsidal (and the font and pulpit are flanking the chancel-arch) it is better not to put the reading desk in the chancel, which best makes its effect free from additional furnishings. The place for the lectern in this type of church is in the nave. It should not stand before or obstruct the chancel, but be near and to the left or right of the font or pulpit.

THE FONT

In the post-Reformation period free standing fonts were not provided for the celebration of the sacrament of baptism in Scottish churches. A metal bracket was fixed near or to the lower part of the pulpit, in which was set a basin, sometimes of silver, more often of pewter, when baptisms were to take place. This was done to give effect to the Reformers' instruction that baptism should be performed publicly and in the face of the Congregation gathered together as a family. Although a special and distinctive font is now almost invariably employed there are examples showing a revival of this pleasant Scottish tradition. Such brackets are usually of wrought-iron which lends itself to graceful and elegant treatment. Normally it should not *look* overheavy, but must be steady.

The majority of the fonts which are to be seen in Scottish churches are made of wood, with an opening in the flat top for the basin which will contain the water. Prior to the Reformation fonts were frequently of stone or marble, which naturally can also be used; with stone, medieval symbolism found an illusion to the rock in the wilderness from which the water issued when struck by Moses. Other materials were also employed: there are Romanesque fonts in England which are made of lead. In Germany a number of examples are fashioned out of bronze.

A free standing font is usually placed flanking the sanctuary opening—perhaps balancing the pulpit or the lectern. An alternative, recently revived, is to form a wall recessed feature, preferably adjacent to the pulpit, somewhat reminiscent of the traditional stoup.

Wherever the font be placed, there are several practical considerations that should be satisfied. While the congregation must be able to witness the sacrament, sufficient clear floor space must be available for the parents, bearing in mind the possibility that several infants may be baptised at any one service. There is much to be said for pouring the water, with the clear, clean sound, from a little ewer into the font bowl during the service. Therefore some ledge or shelf should be to hand for the ewer. A convenient peg or hook to take a draped hand towel will avoid the unseemly effect of a dish-cloth idly discarded.

The exterior shape or container for the bowl of a free standing font can be in a variety of forms, the surface of which may be enriched. The octagon is a usual and satisfactory shape whose sides afford fields for appropriate decoration. These panels may be occupied by symbols of Baptism, the Church or the Holy Spirit. Here, as in other furnishings of the church, the employment of colour in the background can serve to enhance the appearance and assist in throwing the design into more clear relief.

The support, carefully proportioned with the size of the bowl to avoid a top heavy appearance, should always look and be both firm and solid.

The bowl itself which can be quite small, should, of course, be watertight and either lift out for cleaning and emptying or be drainable. As to height a top level of 3 feet 3 inches from the floor beneath will be found convenient. If possible the font can, with benefit, be raised on a 5 inch high step with some 1 foot 9 inches standing width for the minister.

Rather than the plain and unattractive form of a flat board, the cover can also be given dignity and elaboration. The possibilities range from decorative lifting handles to a treatment harking back to those splendid examples which have survived from the Middle Ages. This suggests that on occasions a contemporary translation of these high and decorative features might well be installed with effect in a Scottish church. The old font-covers rose up in the form of spires, enriched and supported by little flying buttresses to which were added finials, crockets and

D

niches, the whole being enlivened with gilding and colour. Attached to a counter-weight by a chain, they could be raised or lowered as required.

FOR a few gathered together for Communion, a small marriage, a commemoration or a discourse, there is a special intimacy that is provided by a side chapel. Associated with the parent church, such a setting also meets the demand for that sense of seclusion which induces private devotion.

Whether the church be new or old, the siting of a chapel requires thought. To be satisfactory, access for both clergy and laity should be simple. An open screen is usually necessary to separate and yet define a tranquil harbour of peace; for occasions of greater privacy this may require the addition of curtains. On the assumption that the space is separated from the church itself by an opening that can be completely infilled by a grille with locking gates, the desirable possibility of an ever-open chapel can be examined. Such a feature pre-supposes that external access can be arranged. Possibilities that can be imagined are either the use of a transept or perhaps the end of a long entrance lobby with the sanctuary within the confines of the church, possibily tucked under a gallery.

The number of chairs to be provided will be a matter of expediency. While less than a dozen may prove useless, a figure which overtops some fifty defeats the purpose. The temptation must be resisted to increase numbers at the expense of generous space between the front row and the Table, since crowding in any form or shape will result not in character but in claustrophobia. Chairs should be widely spaced and hassocks provided.

While the Communion Table must not be small in conception, it need not be large in physical dimension: it must be scaled to the size of the chapel. As it is the focal point, slight elevation to assist vision may be considered. As elsewhere, the Table should be absolutely clear of the non-liturgical: for all specific details, reference should be made to the appropriate section of this work, bearing in mind that, in addition to the clergymen at any service, there will be in all probability no more than two participating elders.

The decorative treatment calls for comment. As the chapel is a part of the greater whole so must it be in complete harmony with the church. But being small it will be subjected to closer scrutiny. Therefore the possibilities arise for the inclusion of even finer jewel-like workmanship. Finely woven tapestry hangings and rugs, more detailed carvings in stone and wood, lettering of great quality—nobly spaced—metal work designed and wrought with love can each have its place. Should painting find a place in the Church of Scotland, the work of the artist is most probably at its happiest here, provided that it is a true work of art, is well placed and does not come in conflict with window glass. This statement is not to be read as encouragement for the inclusion of pictures commercially produced or minded. Nothing could be more unacceptable than the average " sacred " print which, in revealing as much technical accomplishment as sentimentality, has qualities which are neither creative nor spiritual. Let those responsible have the vision and courage to commission paintings, either framed or painted on the wall.

THE AISLES

THE arteries of a church are its aisles which are provided primarily to facilitate circulation and to a lesser degree to subdivide lengths of seating into manageable proportions. It is important that the aisles be direct and wide enough to cope easily with the nature and maximum flow of traffic. While the wider the more satisfying from the visual point of view, the minimum appropriate dimension is governed by purpose. Main aisles should not be less than 5 feet 6 inches wide for weddings and funerals—and related to the clear width of doors— with side aisles having a minimum of 4 feet 6 inches. The best widths will be those scaled to the size of the church. With a "tight" plan it may be necessary to refer to the local bye-laws and fire regulations which apply to assemblies of people within buildings.

The centre aisle inevitably will be processional and can with benefit exceed 5 feet 6 inches. If it is possible to allow 8 feet 6 inches the gain in appearance to the entire church will be most marked—and it will be possible to add additional chairs to either side for special occasions and still leave the accepted clear minimum width of 5 feet 6 inches.

All longitudinal aisles should terminate opposite doors for entry and exit. These should lead direct to draught-preventing vestibules which must be adequate for the rapid emptying of the church. It will also be necessary to plan the disposition of the aisles leading from the vestry and session room, having regard to the movements of the minister, possibly the choir, and most certainly the elders bringing in the Elements for Holy Communion.

As many members have a marked disinclination to reach their seats by approaching in the face of the congregation, the main entrance should serve the church from as far back as possible. And wherever this entrance may be, it is unfortunate if there be no " centre " aisle, at least traversing the foremost block of seats. In the absence of such a route to the sanctuary, ceremony is robbed of much of its impressiveness.

Lateral communications are also necessary. Generous clear space, 6 feet by 8 feet as a minimum, should intervene between the front row of seating and the chancel, sanctuary or pulpit. Such an unencumbered area will also serve to assist hearing as it provides a sound reflector in one of the positions where it is most necessary. It will also be invaluable for marriages, funerals and other ceremonies. It is helpful if there can be a direct route from this point to some retiring room, for the use on those occasions when participants taking part under tension have to withdraw. There should also be an aisle behind the rearmost rows of seats to provide for the movements of elders without necessitating the opening of doors and entry of draughts.

Every effort must be made to avoid ramped aisles or the inclusion of steps. Should the latter be necessary they must be as wide and shallow as possible (say 5 inches by 14 inches) preferably without projecting nosings—and never in groups of less than three.

The best material for surfacing aisles requires thought and decision in the light of prevailing wishes, circumstances and the character sought. Such factors that must be examined are freedom from noise, cleanliness, durability, appearance, acoustic properties and cost.

Undoubtedly good quality carpeting, properly fixed down, which wears reasonably well can be most satisfactory. But inferior qualities and loosely woven materials should be avoided as being lurking places for dirt, disappointing in durability and likely to cause tripping.

Any woven pile material can with benefit have an overall pattern of subdued form or " texture " relief to obviate the unsightliness of footprints. In addition, the discreet rhythm of a repeated motif materially assists in giving " scale ", a note of colour interest, and sense of perspective to the long lines of the aisles.

Linoleum and the plastic tiles now available are serviceable and a good compromise between " soft " and " hard " finishes. The potentialities for simple pattern and choice of colour are great and the layout of the design can be made quite simply for the particular project. The marks of traffic can be conspicuous on self-coloured materials; this unsightliness is minimised if the choice is made from marbled patterns. If laid on an existing floor and not countersunk to the level of the neighbouring surfaces, the edges should be finished flush with protective beads of metal or hardwood.

Rubber shares many of the characteristics of linoleum. In addition, it tends to be slippery under wet feet, and if badly laid can result in " creep ", giving a wrinkled surface.

In either boarding or block form, hardwood, lovely in itself, may not be perfect for circulation spaces. It will require greater and constant maintenance: being resonant, particularly when laid as strip flooring on battens it will tend to magnify rather than suppress sound. On occasions boards are prone to squeak.

The cheapest finish is granolithic concrete. For a church this workshop surface has against it every characteristic other than economy. It is drab—in spite of all the colour agents which can be added. It is dirty in its " dusting "—in spite of all the chemical hardeners which must be renewed from time to time. It is so " hard " as to be particularly noisy. When used, it should be divided into compartments by the use of incised " joints " or inlayed strips. Even so, it *can* part company with its substruction if badly laid or insufficiently " keyed ": where this occurs there may be unsightly patching.

Many are the " jointless " floor coverings now available. These are satisfactory on a concrete substructure provided there is no subsidence or structural movement. According to formula and mix they vary from " semi soft " to hard. Attractive colours are available and in many cases they can be laid to a design. The available and suitable types are best discussed with an architect.

Stone flags, slate, marble and tiles each have their qualities and attractions. The intrinsic worth of the material demands careful choice and design. Where appropriate their inclusion goes far to give dignity associated with the character of formality. Such materials may raise queries regarding comfort, additional carpeting, sound—and cost.

As practically every floor will require periodic mechanical treatment—vacuum cleaners or polishers—a sufficient number of 15 amp electric power points should be fitted to avoid over-long trailing flexes.

IF they are to plan satisfactory buildings, those who are called upon to design churches must be made familiar with the uses of all the accommodation. A few notes may not come amiss on the purposes of all the additional rooms that will be requested.

Vestry. This room is basically the minister's office which he also uses for robing. It should be accessible from outside through a vestibule and be near the session room. It must have privacy. Entered through a ventilated lobby there should be a lavatory and washhand basin with hot water readily to hand.

When in the church it is here that the minister will see his visitors and make arrangements with them. Space is required for a desk and a table as wedding parties may sign the register in this room. The minister will possibly conduct very small classes in his vestry, which calls for some additional chairs. He will require shelves for a limited number of books and the furnishing must include a full-length mirror and hanging cupboards for robes, coats and hats and possibly a safe. Good general external and internal local lighting along with some form of easily regulated heating will be essential.

The placing of the vestry which must be directly connected with the church itself should be discussed with the minister or committee. The decision, which will be governed by intentions regarding entry and exit, may affect the use of the room for those signing the marriage register.

The Session Room is the business centre of the church community. It must be large enough to seat the entire kirk session and the board of management, when this is additional, at their meetings. Provision should be allowed for possible expansion in numbers. With a small session, the members may sit around a table, but otherwise it is more economic in floor space to arrange them in rows. With his session clerk beside him, the minister, possibly gowned, will preside as moderator of the session. The entrance must therefore be convenient for the vestry, and the moderator's table be sensibly sited; at the end opposite the door makes for the convenience of latecomers and early leavers.

As the session room will be used independently it must have its separate external access which it can well share with the vestry accommodation. It must also connect with the church, preferably at the same level and via an intervening lobby.

The office-bearers will congregate here before and after services. It is in this room that they will perform tasks as varied as arranging the Elements for the Communion Service and counting the collection, both of which require good table space with free surrounding floor. Many kirk sessions require a safe. Good cupboard space is essential to store the inevitable accumulation of papers, spare service books, general literature and multifarious articles ranging from the Christmas tree lights to the collection bags. Hat and coat pegs are better placed in the corridor or lobby outside.

Inevitably the room will be used day and night as a place of meeting for many of the congregational committees and classes. It must therefore have good general lighting (natural and artificial), heating which can be regulated, curtains or blinds for the windows, and means of ventilation.

Ladies' Room. Wherever possible this should be provided. It has many uses ranging from regular Sunday use by the lady members of the choir to a place of refuge for the faint. It requires a full-length couch and a mirror. If it can be arranged, a private lavatory will be appreciated. This can well be approached by an ante-room fitted with a deep sink, cupboards and a table for the purposes of those enthusiasts who are responsible for flowers. It should also have such drawered fitments as may be necessary to contain pulpit falls, Communion Table covers, book markers, vases, etc. The architect who designs this room and its fittings without reference to the ladies concerned does so at his peril. (*Note*: this accommodation may not be required should the church proper be linked directly to the hall and its associated rooms).

Lavatories for congregational use by both sexes should be available. With careful planning those already mentioned should be convenient.

The Vestibule or Porch. As the main entrance to the church and all its accommodation, this place of transit is important if for no reason other than that it assists in introducing the character of the interior to which it gives access. It should be light, attractive and inviting.

While there must be provision for vehicles easily to draw up and pull away as close as possible to the entrance doors, the road connections are better off a main throughfare to avoid congestion. The possibility for car parking on an increasingly generous scale must also be examined and if necessary provided. As there will be much opening and closing of doors, the external orientation is best away from the direction of the prevailing wind. Generous floor mats, let flush into the floor, over which the incoming *must* walk will materially assist in maintaining a clean church. As wedding and funeral processions will marshal and disperse in the vestibule there must be adequate space for movement and turning.

Those on duty will take up their stance in this vestibule to welcome visitors, hand out service books and supervise retiring collections. They should be protected from draughts and will require small tables for spare books and perhaps alms dishes.

Cases can well be included for the bulk storage of service books, and racks be provided for the sale and distribution of church literature.

The minister may wish to speed his flock on its way at the

conclusion of the service, and it is here that he will then be. As at the best of times a congregation is slow to disperse there must be room for those who wish to linger and talk without obstructing the main flow of outgoing people.

Should there be a gallery for choir or congregation, the access stair will be in or directly off the vestibule.

EVERY church which acknowledges the comprehensive nature of Divine Service understands the importance of the contribution made by music. Were the choir to do no more than lead congregational singing a great need would be fulfilled. Fortunately there are many church choirs whose contribution far exceeds the bounds of this bare minimum.

Having acknowledged fully the importance of music in the congregational life, the matter must be seen in correct proportion: while it is important, it is not all-important. As no church must sacrifice its greater purpose to become a concert hall, the placing of organ and choir demands earnest thought. The organist, who will rightly be consulted, is by no means the best or only person to give the final decision on this matter since it is not impossible that he may be anxious to obtain for his department over-much prominence in the face of the congregation. It is wise also to remember that however long his tenure may be it will terminate and that his successor may have different ideas. . . . It must also be admitted that, while expressing gratitude for the generous services given so readily, the choir may not always be a visual asset to the church. And it must be conceded that there may be organists who, finding themselves by fortune or design in a prominent position, have to be subjected to restraint; it is unnecessary for them to provide a spectacular display in the name of leading unaccompanied anthems and congregational singing.

The decision as to location will obviously be governed greatly by the shape of the church and the size of both choir and instrument. There is one position alone in the Church of Scotland which is unacceptable under any circumstances: that is to interpose the organ, organist and choir between Communion Table and congregation. In England this so-called but erroneous "medieval" arrangement became all too familiar as a consequence of the Oxford Movement in the nineteenth century. The practice rapidly spread to new churches in Scotland where such planning has no relevance whatsoever in the corporate worship that is the contribution of the Reformed tradition.

In the case of a new church, although the organ may not be installed for a period of years, it is desirable to have it fully designed at the outset. It is only in this way that there will be an accurate and economic disposition of space which can make allowance also for any possible future extensions. As the size of the instrument will be related to the cost, this indicates a budget. Subsequent deviation will lead to dissatisfaction since reduction leads to insufficiency, and increase, other than planned additions, to a lack of balance.

The placing will be considered relative to function. It is essential, save only in most exceptional circumstances, that the console, the sounding portion of the instrument and the choir should be closely associated with each other to enable the organist, in exercising control, to hear the blended sounds simultaneously. To be certain of his cues the organist must also be able to see the minister. It is best if the sight lines can be direct to the Communion Table, the pulpit and, if possible, the lectern and font. While it is most helpful if he can be in the same relationship to the principal entrance for processional occasions, he may have to be content with mirror, bell, buzzer or phone.

It is possible musically to place choir and organ outside and behind the sanctuary: as this placing can easily lead to unwarranted dramatic effects, seemliness may well demand complete screening from congregational view. But further: in the Reformed Church, the choir and organist are part of the congregation and the sense of this unity should be preserved both during the choir's singing and silence.

Wherever they are to be placed, it is best acoustically if there can be no obstacle between choir and organ on the one hand, and both of these and the congregation on the other.

At times the front rows of the nave are used to seat the choir. Everything possible must be done to discourage this placing. While no doubt it is theoretically satisfactory, the solution may create more problems than it solves. No choir can lead from this position. The performance of an anthem will be ridiculous if the singers do not turn round to face the congregation—and when they do, the consequences are unfortunate in the extreme both visually and aurally for those sitting near. It must be noted that this is one of the two locations which can result in an unacceptable console position; being central and perhaps sunk in front of the Communion Table and possibly pulpit, it merely obstructs practically, visually and processionally. The second location for the choir with similar consequences occurs in those churches which, with axially placed consoles, permit the borrowing of the elders' space in the sanctuary area. It is unseemly to tolerate any such intrusion into the area of consecration: it also implies the removal of the choir to liberate the space for its rightful use on the occasion of Communion. Neither of these two positions should be accepted in a new church—and those older buildings that are arranged in this fashion should strive to give effect to modifications at the very earliest opportunity.

It may be, through the exigencies of the building or for any other reason, that the choir and organist must be sited in such a way that they separate the Communion Table from the congregation. Under these circumstances, two or three rows of chairs (or preferably enclosed pews) *can* be arranged facing inwards and towards each other following the collegiate plan. There should be an 8 foot wide centre aisle with 5 foot cross passages parting both congregation from choir, and choir from sanctuary. The organ console should be located within the confines of the choir enclosure thus formed. It is best placed at the sanctuary end, abutting on the centre aisle, with the organist facing across, at 90 degrees to the main axis of the church. But it is to be noted that the choir will function all the better undivided. The musical results—the blending of sound and the supporting singing—will be improved with the foregoing arrangement confined either to the left or to the right of the church.

Conditional on the shape of the building a more acceptable and workable solution is to situate the choir and organ in front of the congregation but well to the left or right as may be appropriate, facing across the church. The most simple example is one of the transepts of a cruciform plan. Provided that there is space enough for the organ and its chamber, of shortcomings this position appears to have none, the advantages being so obvious that comment is superfluous. The choir can, with profit, be elevated on a timber staged sound box platform, perhaps some 4 feet above general floor level with the organ itself free-standing across the transept gable. For this layout the optimum position for the console is at the " west " end, tucked behind the return wall of the transept so that the organist faces both Table and pulpit beyond the choir seats.

An ample shallow chamber fully open to the church on the north or south (or both) transept or nave walls should be provided for the sounding portion of the organ, with the mouths of the speaking pipes preferably 12 to 15 feet but certainly not less than 6 feet above the floor of the church. There should be at least 2 feet clear above the top of the tallest pipe to allow it to speak. Should there be sufficient space in the nave, transepts or at the sides of the sanctuary—and funds—a free standing organ case will provide better results musically and a more splendid opportunity for architectural expression. Nevertheless, any case work enclosing the pipes reduces the output of sound. Many organs are now built, with satisfactory decorative results, in which the pipes and other essential parts of the organ are freely displayed in their functional arrangements.

It is a concensus of opinion throughout Christendom that where they occur, west galleries provide the best position of all for both choir and organ. This is now a twentieth century classic solution and many lovely examples from all denominations can be cited. In this position the organ pipes do not intrude themselves, the choir can be suitably grouped near the organist and the construction of the gallery itself, which should not be too high above the nave floor, forms an effective sound-box. Should there be any suggestion of musical objection to such " relegation " it may be assumed that it can only be based on a healthy arrogance which persuasion should overcome. A further objection that has been voiced is that this position for the choir adversely affects recruiting—a matter which can surely be left safely to the enthusiasm of the organist and those who want to sing. Of all positions, it is from here that the choir can best lead.

In laying out seating it is well to remember that the choir requires comfort. The dimensions for each person from side to side and from front to back should be generous (2 feet wide by 3 feet deep). It must be borne in mind that with many churches, in which the choir is in the face of the congregation, there is a growing desire to add to the minimum seemliness with the use of robes. Undoubtedly with appreciation and understanding this desire will grow: a robed choir requires greater room and it is therefore imprudent to cramp these surroundings.

It will be appreciated that the choir can be accommodated in pews, if need be stepped up. The book boards should be sized to take sheet music at a height convenient (about 3 feet 6 inches from floor) for use when the singers stand. As this height, which can probably be made to accord with the console, may obstruct vital congregational sight lines, the placing must be carefully verified.

The position selected for the choir will have implications on

E

the treatment to be given to the organ and its case if the instrument is to be contained. The decorative expression will also be governed by possible expenditure and both the nature and scale of the organ, which now must be considered.

A pipe organ consists of three departments: (i) the wind supply consisting of the blower, one or more reservoirs and the ducts, (ii) the sound chest carrying the pipes and (iii) the console containing the manual, pedal keyboards and the stop controls. While various arrangements are possible the simplest and most economic is to have the wind supply beneath the sound chest and the console attached to the front. All the parts must be readily accessible for maintenance several times a year. The instrument should be built against a wall to gain the maximum benefit of sound reflection and physical support.

The matter is so important that any congregation requiring a new organ must seek expert professional advice. The general recommendation is that normally the best choice will be a purpose-built pipe organ which need not be large. A small instrument with balanced tone quality will lead praise far more effectively than will be possible with a larger thick and heavy toned organ. Although it is highly desirable to have a two-manual organ on which practically all organ music can be played, not only to enrich the congregational musical life but also to fulfil its duties as a teaching instrument, in straightened circumstances one manual can serve adequately. It is better to have a really good single-manual instrument than an inferior one with two manuals.

In selecting an organ there are various possibilities open. Best of all is the purpose-made instrument which may or may not include in its specification standardised units, and if so desired second-hand parts. It is constructed both musically and architecturally to suit the building it is to serve. An important point is that it can also be planned easily to take future extensions which should be envisaged at the outset. A second choice lies in ready-made extension pipe organs which are made by a number of firms. More or less satisfactory, they are not ideal from the musical point of view. The principal architectural difficulty is that, being prefabricated, they cannot be altered to suit surroundings without disproportionate expense. Second-hand instruments have the same drawbacks with the added difficulty that they have been designed for acoustic surroundings in every probability very different from the proposed new setting. The cost of the necessary internal and external alterations, when added to the purchase price, can bring the total up to or beyond the purchase price of a new instrument—and provide an organ with a shorter working life.

It is suggested that any who are contemplating an electronic organ should also obtain an estimate for a small but adequate " straight " pipe organ. It is probable that the costs will not be notably different. Doubtless any who insist on this step will be informed by those who would not dream of sapping the vitality of the Bible by expurgation that there is no difference between the quality of the sounds produced by a pipe organ on the one hand and an electronic instrument on the other. Indeed, it is difficult to appreciate why a particular kind of sound should be so sacrosanct that, in the absence of the genuine, there are so many prepared to accept a less satisfactory sham. Under such circumstances the reasoning is that which is unable to discriminate between a carillon and recorded bells, between a commercially produced print and an original work for the side chapel and between the mass produced and perhaps mechanically ornamented chancel furnishings and the work of a craftsman. There is a difference—the difference that distinguishes Truth from Falsehood—over which there must be no compromise. In the electronic instrument, the sounds of organ pipes are copied (with varying fidelity) and are amplified through loudspeakers. While opinions vary on their merits most musicians dislike them and congregations find the " dead " tone palls. Their ability to lead and support congregational singing—the principal purpose of the organ—is very much open to question. It must also be appreciated that the techniques of sound reproduction are at present under rapid development. Current methods may be superseded in the near future: this will mean that a model new to-day will rapidly become obsolete and that instead of repairs there will be replacement. All avenues must be explored before an electronic instrument is accepted; as a last resort congregations might at least seek competent advice and even study the possibilities of a piano. Only those who have heard such an instrument in ecclesiastical surroundings can know how fine the results can be.

The electronic instrument does not raise decorative problems, as it merely requires the decency of grilles to mask speakers. The casing of a pipe organ is another matter. Governed by position, setting, scale and funds, the treatment for the " kist o' whistles " can range from the unembellished ranges of exposed pipes that have been mentioned or the simplest possible wood-work to the elaborate vehicle for splendid and superb decoration. The pipes themselves should be handled sympathetically. The traditional organ pipe " spotted metal " is an alloy of most attractive character, being mottled with textural markings and gleaming in appearance. A congregation is fortunate to possess an organ with such pipes, which, wax polished, should be preserved in their natural state. The natural colour for organ pipes is silver-grey; where zinc pipes occur it is necessary to coat the surfaces for which a pewter coloured lead paint should be used. Along with plush and stencilled wall decoration the painted patterning that gave to a range of pipes the appearance of rolls of linoleum should not be repeated. Gone also is gilt. Were the surfaces to be treated with gold leaf, burnished to afford brilliant high lights and sombre darks there could be splendour: but unfortunately the gold paint that is applied with a brush or sprayed has not the unique character and normally is better avoided.

In present times no church will be designed with the organ pipes rising high and cliff like behind a central pulpit. But many existing churches are furnished in this manner to the point of appearing and being overcrowded and overpowering. Such churches should endeavour to liberate their sanctuaries and gain quiet empty space by internal reconstruction: the potentialities for improvement to the dignity of the services and visual satisfaction can exceed expectation.

THE pages of this book make no claim to originality. The sole intention is to provide in a convenient form the essential requirements and the ways and means by which our churches may be brought to sing their part in the universal message of joy, hope and comfort. Success, never easy, can best be achieved when a clear statement of the fundamental data is used creatively by a trained and sensitive designer. It is then, and possibly only then, that the church can achieve the synthesis that is the co-ordination of the multifarious—and at times conflicting—interests and come to express itself as a symphony of form and colour that can be and is loved by its users.

Tradition has enriched the church not only with choir and organ, but also with the music of peel, chime and toll. As rousing as silver trumpets, bells—the word is derived from the Saxon *bellan*, to bellow or make a noise—have their full eloquence in moments of gladness and sadness. On an historic May Day, Edinburgh heard the St Giles' bells peal forth in celebration of the Treaty of Union in 1707: " Why should I be sad on my Wedding Day ". These pages would indeed be incomplete were they to be without reference to a subject which is so closely associated with the Church.

For a thousand years in our land men have built the House of God standing in the very heart of the community. By its nature the church was usually more lofty and large than the surrounding homes of the parish it was designed to serve. Whether the church took its place in the street scene or was withdrawn within its own grounds, perhaps graced with the privacy of fine trees, the emphasis, if only through size, was one of dominance. That these buildings, transmuted by skill, faith and love into architecture, were frequently ennobled with the upward thrust of towers was not only a satisfactory foil to the horizontal lines of roof and wall: towers were added purposefully to house the bells.

It is little wonder that there are so few pre-Reformation bells. Many must have been lost in fires. Others are known to have been an all too convenient source of revenue or gunmetal; it will be recalled in this connection that in medieval times the great bell of a major ecclesisatical building was usually the property of the burghers (as were all of a collegiate church) who therefore acted as they thought best with their own property. In every possibility with antiquarian interest surpassing musical quality many of the surviving bells were either replaced or recast to meet the demands for improved quality of sound and interval that came with the introduction of change ringing in the seventeenth century of which a full description based on 5, 6, 8, 10 or 12 bells tuned to a major scale has no place here. Let it be sufficient to note that it has been calculated how, with 5 bells, 24 changes occupying one minute can be rung: with the full scale of 12 bells over 479 million are possible, occupying 38 years all but 5 days. . . .

It is beyond doubt that bells as we know them were an early invention of the Christian church. While it is likely that they were originally used to summon the worshippers in the happier days that replaced early persecution, the first record of a bell left to us dates from the ninth century. In the Middle Ages casting was frequently local, but later burgh records indicate that great store was then set on the skill of the founders of Flanders. The creation of a successful bell has always demanded knowledge and skill of a high order as can be inferred from a brief technical description.

To amplify the dictionary, a bell can be defined as being a hollow, pulsating body of cast metal, being of deep cup shape widening at the lip, which, when sounded percussively, emits a musical sound of a definite pitch. It is essential that the body be elastic, tough and durably hard for which the most suitable metal has been found to be bronze. The best alloy, by the experience of tradition, consists of 13 parts of copper to 4 of tin. It is the function of the latter to add density and hardness to the sonority of the former. On these occasions when bells have been cast in steel, they have been found to be not only easy victims of corrosion, but also deficient in tonal quality and carrying power. The success of a bell, which so far has eluded scientific explanation, is governed by the niceties of metallic purity, shape and the relationships of height, width and wall thickness. It is the bell founder's pride that he achieves, through perfection of contour and proportion, true qualities of tune and tone, which are not synonymous. The attributes that make for successful tone lie in the fact that there are at least five distinct notes brought into being when any bell is sounded. When correctly struck the initial sound which attracts the ear is the strike note, tap or fundamental. When this has lost its first intensity, the ear can discern the hum note, an octave lower. Dependent on the size of the bell two or more further harmonics also come into play. The skill of the founders can be appreciated when it is realised that each of these over and under tones must be separately and perfectly tuned.

The secrets of successful founding, with the tolerances necessary for, and the means of, final five tone tuning are not to be found in text books; the empirical experiences of years are handed from generation to generation. It is with regret that the recent closing of Scotland's sole foundry has to be recorded. However, Europe's largest and most perfectly equipped firm for the making of bells is at Loughborough.

Bells are no longer sounded for curfew, to warn of fire or approaching enemy—or, along with book and candle, part of the ritual of excommunication. Nevertheless any possibility for their inclusion in a Scottish church must be encouraged to give general and outward expression of joy, to summon, to sound the passing hours . . . and with muffled tones to toll for the departed. In planning for their inclusion there are four important and general considerations. First, in our mechanised age which facilitates so-called reproduction, the available substitutes all too often are cheaper (which has appeal to the undiscerning) and less satisfactory by far (which is clear to the knowledgeable). Invading the realms of everyday life and embracing the visual arts and music, this degeneration can threaten the church in many ways. The electronic system implies amplification which can introduce the distortion that arises from the introduction of the machine. Whether or not a deception such as this can be detected by the trained or untrained ear, such an installation is and remains a fake. As such it has no place in the church and must be eschewed. Second, the bells must be hung as high as possible above the level of surrounding roofs and trees to permit the blending and spreading of the sound. It is of course to direct the sound waves downwards that belfry openings traditionally are infilled with stone, slate or hardwood louvres. But sight must not be lost of the decorative potential latent in the bells themselves being exposed to view. Third, in order to create its note, the heavy bell itself either is swung or is struck to chime. In both cases vibration to a greater or lesser degree is created. It is therefore advisable that all details for the design of the actual belfry should be prepared in full consultation with the bell founders who will appreciate this co-operation at as early a stage as possible. And lastly, the regular chiming of bells can be disturbing. It should be verified, therefore, that there is no hospital or other institution in the immediate neighbourhood that is likely in any way to suffer.

The means used for sounding will be considered relative both to the space requirements and to the method used for suspension. Whether they be contained in a cote integral with the design of a gable, in a decorative *flèche* overriding the ridge of a roof or are placed within a belfry chamber crowning a tower, the bells themselves must be accessible. They are sounded by being struck, either on the outside near the lower rim by hammer or mallet, or by the swinging movement of the metal clapper. In the former instance the operation can be mechanically governed by a clock and for a sufficiency of bells it is possible to include a keyboard. This can be played by hand or operated automatically. For bell-ringers the chamber requires a minimum height of 12 feet which should be separated from the belfry floor by an air space of at least 2 feet 6 inches. In the case of the bell that is sounded manually from ground or low level, protection for the ringer will be appreciated. Whether outside, within the porch or inside the church itself this indicates the use of a weather-proofed sleeve. This is to permit the passage through the roof construction of the cord or chain to which a water-shedding metal protective cone must be fitted as close as possible to the opening. It will not come amiss, experience has taught, for the free end of the bell-pull to be made lockfast in a narrow " cupboard " whose top is out of normal reach.

The value to many churches of the emphasis provided by tower or steeple will be appreciated readily. In terms of architectural form, the designer of the building, should he seek the vertical, will best determine the character. In this connection it is tempting to enquire why architects of to-day do not again turn to the potentialities of the dome for larger churches. A contemporary interpretation of this noble architectural feature, which bears a most illustrious pedigree, would appear to be a fitting dominant and outward expression of the centralised planning that suits the church of to-day. Towers, whether integrated to the main fabric of the building or on an open site free-standing in the Italian manner which runs as an unbroken tradition from the Early Christian days, may be clothed in walls, sturdy or fine. Or they may be delicately designed as an open pattern of lattice work with interest and play of line from all viewpoints. From its simple, practical origins the function

of the tower now extends far beyond the mere physical supporting of bells and the essential lightning-conductor, which, to
bring the subject momentarily down to earth, should travel in
the straightest possible line and avoid sharp bends from its
antenna on the highest point down to a large copper plate
buried deep beneath the foundations. Should the tower no
longer be necessary for us to mount the nightly watch, it nevertheless stands to remind us that it is the Church which at all times
stands guard over us. In their moments of aspiration men have
ever built upwards; there must be few who, in their humility,
fail to respond in their own way to the call of their faith as when

> Old de Wyvil built a spire,
> That men could see across the shire:
> All he thought, he could not say
> When he knelt him down to pray:
> When his soul with music filled,
> He could not sing—but he could build.
> So he took his measuring rod,
> And he built a spire to God.*

* That I am unable to make acknowledgement for these words torn from a news-
paper when serving overseas during the war, I regret. I know neither author nor
source.   E. G.

SYMBOLS AND SYMBOLISM

THERE are Misters, Esqs., Drs and perhaps even Revs. who are of the opinion that symbolism has no place within the Reformed Church. Yet the bearers of these titles will doff their hats, shake hands, stand for the National Anthem and would be affronted were they not to give their brides wedding rings in church. Entering our lives at every turn, symbols are to be found in the very streets we use, from the chemists shop to coats of arms, from road-signs to monuments and memorials. A symbol, however lowly or lovely it may be, is that which, by general consent, is charged with analogous meaning. It is of little consequence that the full implications may not be understood by all. The symbol is also a vehicle which adds to graciousness and which associates us with the stream of life that has travelled down from past ages to reach us of to-day. To ignore the latent possibilities is deliberately to cut ourselves off from much of significance, interest and beauty.

When used in ecclesiastical buildings, symbols group themselves into three categories:

> Those that *must* be incorporated into the building, such as the Cross of our Lord, and the Holy Table.
>
> Those that can be induced to give an added significance to that which is essential—for example the nave, the placing of the font, the cruciform shape of a church and the weathervane.
>
> And lastly—which are more the concern of this handbook—those which we use to hold the interest at focal points and give reasons with meaning to enrichment. In themselves they are equally important for their intrinsic worth and their underlying message.

The most prolific users of symbolism were the medieval church builders from whom much can be learned that is to our profit. Without enlarging on the way that windows and carvings brought the well-loved tales to a population unable to read, it will be accepted that of all five senses, vision is that which best makes an imprint on the retentive memory. The medieval men, conscious or unconscious of this fact when they built, did not merely place stone upon stone—they constructed idea.

Forms in themselves are meaningless and imagination is given to us as one of the greatest manifestations of religious force. The designers and craftsmen of the Middle Ages created a new world of the mind as vivid and intense as that in which they laboured. In terms of symbols they carved the angels in the heights of the roof construction and they placed Christ in judgement above the west door. The figures they created were not dead idols, they were profound, moving and therefore living symbols. The world these men knew and loved gave them the inspiration for the foliated and flowered caps and bosses, while comment on everyday life is to be found carved on misericord seats. No less pungent and necessary to the medieval mind was Limbo: as a foil and contrast that accentuates both the glories of the celestial hereafter and the present life on earth, it is little wonder that the nether world also had its place. Hence Satan, the little devils, imps and grotesques which are thoughtlessly admired to-day as being merely " quaint ".

Thus the use of symbols in white stone, sombre timber, gleaming glass, in a setting enlivened with gold and rich colour made of the church a framework of parables that impressed themselves indelibly on the memory: they form a complete expression and commentary on a very real concept and philosophy of life.

No suggestion is intended that we should indulge in medievalism or indeed any superabundance of richness in our buildings to-day. Nevertheless where emphasis is required this is still

achieved by providing a focal point—something to see. Whereas
the architect may say that all he seeks is light and shade to
punctuate, others will seek a note of interest. A true designer of
a church will gladly accept this opportunity whenever he can
and satisfy these wishes in a way that is redolent with meaning.

In ecclesiastical symbolism it takes little study to reveal that
much which we accept is prechristian in origin. It is none the
worse for that. That such signs were adopted by the Church in
the wisdom of its early days is of great importance. In the world
which saw the last days of the Roman Empire in the west and
the rise of Constantinople, the tradition to spreading Christianity
was smoothed by the deliberate and wise continuation of existing
rites and customs under a new guise.

In the early days of the Church's history long known
attributes of unemployed members of the Pantheon were
grafted on to New Testament personalities to make them more
readily acceptable and understood. St Peter now carries the keys
that were formerly in the keeping of Janus, while Satan, as we
recognise him, is Pan in disguise. Venus and Cupid clothed and
reformed themselves to continue their claim on attentive devotion. While the tonsure was adopted from India, incense was
used with reluctance at the outset because of its pagan associations.
From the dates of Christmas and Easter to the forms of infant
baptism, the marriage service and funerals we find origins and
practices that antedate Christianity. With little research it is easy
to see how the stream swells to become that broad fast flowing
river of unplumbable depth which links us directly with our
remote ancestors.

The supreme symbol within the church *must* be the Cross
of Our Lord: Here also are inspiring derivations and changes
in significance. It was already familiar in Egypt as Tau, the sign
used in associations of great learning; its adoption as the Sign of
Christian faith, first made by Constantine, was no innovation.
At the outset the Sign stood for Unity, the One was All in All,

the full implications of the suffering of the Crucifixion coming later in time. The development of the portrayal of Our Lord, from the earliest static figure with sublime expression of repose and with outstretched arms against no Cross whatsoever to the tortured realism of the agonies which came in the Renaissance days, unfortunately has no place in this book. In the Church of Scotland it is the form alone, the significant brooding Cross, which dominates. The use must be restricted, for it is an error to reduce the impact by over-indulgence.

As the most important appointment within the church, the Communion Table is an obvious field for allegorical enrichment. With thought and imagination it is possible to find symbols other than the hackneyed vegetation of vine and wheat. An Early Christian representation shows loaves and fishes as indicative, not of the Miracle, but of the Supper; from the same source comes the chalice and cross-marked wafer. Two doves drinking from a chalice also date from the very early centuries. The Agnus Dei—early representations have a Cross on the head and no nimbus—is of course appropriate. But perhaps most fitting of all are those chosen from the traditional signs for the last hours of Our Lord's life on Earth, being the Lantern and the Torch, with, for the suffering, the Crown of Thorns and the Cross, the three Nails, the Hammer, the Pincers, the Sponge and Reed, the Three Dice and the letters I.N.R.I. Used either jointly with those of the Passion or independently, an emblem for the Resurrection has the forms as the Lion, the Phoenix (which is to be found in the catacombs) the Peacock and the Pelican—the last named when *vulning* herself being emblematic of the Crucifixion. Should the Trinity be considered, it is well to avoid as naive the Romanesquelike use of figures and incorporate either three interlinked circles or two interpenetrating triangles.

Next in importance will be the font. The only known Early Christian symbol used in this connection is one of infinite meaning—the Fish. This came into use in the fourth century, when it was found that the initial letters in Greek for Jesus Christ, Son of God, Saviour spelled out *Ichthus*, the fish. It was frequently used in association with the Dove or the Anchor, the latter being yet a further pagan symbol that was adopted by the primitive Church. There are, of course, further implications not only to the frequent references to fishes in our Lord's life but also to baptismal water and the Church's net. At times three fish were used, forming an entwined triangle which added the significance of the Trinity to baptism.

The familiar Descending Dove indicative of the coming of the Holy Spirit obviously has its ancestry in this important event. The word " Dove " itself contributes to the association if the derivation from the old English " Dufan "—dip or dive—be accepted. A metal Descending Dove over the font was frequently used to contain the Holy Oil formerly used in Baptism and for the administration of Extreme Unction.

Perhaps we can seek further inspiration from medieval times. There are examples of metaphorical baptisms being portrayed— the Fall, the Noah with his Ark and one singularly fine Romanesque font shows appropriately and charmingly the entire legend of St Nicholas.

To examine every article of furnishing—from the lectern and the organ case to the pew end and *prie-Dieu*—in the context of appropriate emblematic treatment would be burdensome to this work. The clergyman, who should have such information as part of his stock-in-trade, must be able to guide the artist seeking an appropriate subject as a significant and interesting vehicle for his decoration.

As potential and appropriate possibilities—the list as will be seen is by no means exhaustive—brief mention is made of the following:

The four Evangelists. Originally shown as four Scrolls, open Books or the four Rivers, the conventional representation became, as is well known, the Man (St Matthew who gives Christ's genealogy), the Lion (St Mark who shows the strength and dignity of Christ), the Ox (St Luke who enlarges on Christ's priesthood and sacrifice) and the Eagle (St John who soars heavenward)—all being winged. The first authority for the use of these symbols is attributed to St Jerome, their derivation from the Scriptures being tenuous since Ezekiel gave each four heads, and in the Book of Revelation, St John tells how each was full of eyes before and behind.

The emblems for the apostles and early saints (frequently the instruments of their martyrdom alone will be seen as, in Scotland, the Cross of St Andrew). Much appropriate and interesting material is to be found in the narratives of the saints of the Celtic Church. Allusion is also possible to many of the saints by reference to their floral tributes.

It is curious that the Church of Scotland should find its symbol, the Burning Bush, from the Old Testament. As an *idea* it is perhaps satisfactory but in execution it has technical difficulties. Success depends entirely on the adequate portrayal of flames, and flames are in essence light, movement and animation.

The Escalop Shell is indicative of the pilgrim and pilgrimage. The lamp or flaming torch represents wisdom and piety. An open Pomegranate alludes to the hope of immortality and the future life.

While weapons of war should normally have no place in the church, there are exceptions. The Sword, either alone or crowned represents the Church Militant; as an instrument of martyrdom it is St Paul's emblem. In St Mark's, Venice, the more modern framework of a Byzantine Madonna displays with realism a rifle carved on the left hand side.

The Ship, of which there are many splendid examples, stands for the Church. One of the oldest symbols is the Tree of Life which Christianity has frequently interpreted as being

F

the Vine. The list of possibilities continues with many more, including the Bell, the Heart (unembellished, flaming, pierced or broken and bound), the Lily, the Star, the Trumpet, and by no means least, but appropriately last, Alpha and Omega.

The Nimbus, the halo, is so universal that it must be mentioned. In the context of ecclesiastical work it is now indicative of sanctity but it was not thus in origin. Of almost universal application—the Classical World, Ancient Egypt, India and the Orient—it came to signify divinity in both this life and in the next. In Christianity it does not appear earlier than the sixth century. The circle (occasionally triangular) distinguished those who had died, the living being indicated by a square nimbus with the lower line parallel with the shoulders. A contained Cross was used to indicate the Saviour alone. On sculptured figures used externally, the halo was designed also to serve the very practical use of providing a protective hood.

Heraldry provides a convenient and terse means of symbolic commemoration which has great decorative possibilities. It must be well designed to have life and distinction. A medieval treatment should not be placed in classical surroundings. Armorial bearings are precise, and it is all to easy to err: in the case of the slightest doubt regarding rectitude the details should be confirmed.

So far as concerns colour, this section would not be complete without reference to the canonical sequence. There is every encouragement for the more widespread dressing of the Holy Table and the use of the correct colours both on pulpit falls and lectern markers.

GREEN   Used on all normal occasions signifies, through the association with Spring, life on earth.

RED   Symbolic of the Passion, is used during Pentecost and can appropriately represent Martyrs.

PURPLE   Indicative of sorrow, has associations with suffering, humility and truth. It is displayed throughout Lent, Holy Week and Advent except on any feast days which might call for an alternative colour.

WHITE   Representing purity and joy is displayed at Christmas, Epiphany and on Easter Sunday.

BLACK   Is occasionally used on Good Friday.

It is hoped that sufficient has now been said to show that by the use of symbols the message of the Church is made more intense and the building more meaningful, lovelier and distinctive. Perhaps generated by subconscious fear, the neglect of the opportunities that God provides for significance and beauty is neither Christian nor sensible. Are we all not prepared to accept without question, as the conclusion of each service, that the Benediction be delivered, with the right hand raised, to be followed by the chords of the concluding AMEN?

COLOUR

No matter what materials may be used in construction there is nothing which does more to determine the character of a church interior than its " colour ". The word is used not in the narrow sense of pink, grey or blue, the paint which comes out of a decorator's tin, but to convey the significance of that carefully balanced symphony, the notes, phrases and movements of which lie in the walls, the furnishings, the windows, the hangings and all else that is within the church. The aim is consciously to create in the minds of others a pre-determined and harmonious mood, in a word, to *design* the colour scheme.

The analogy with music may be carried further. In all great works the elemental theme is invariably simplicity itself: the great composer is he who, in developing these few notes, can invert, elaborate, extend and construct his exposition and harmonies so that we are presented with a work of genius. The scheme for church decoration should have the same elemental simplicity which offers full scope for imaginative variations.

For the colour scheme of a church there are three main considerations over which there may or may not be control.

First. The notes that are to be used in the composition. There are the visual effects of the materials to many of which the building may already be committed. These might well be stone and hardwoods, textiles and glass that cannot or ought not to be changed; the colour scheme must be constructed so that these existing elements all play their parts and contribute to the harmony.

Second. The mood. To a great extent this will inevitably be governed by the nature of the interior, and it will be courting disaster should, for example, any attempt be made to force a brilliantly lit, delicately detailed Georgian church to assume an air of mysterious grandeur. What is *there*, be the church new or old, will go far to establish the mood or character. Accepting this limitation as a source of inspiration, decision must then be made as to the pitch to which the development may be lifted . . . it must even be decided whether the key be major or minor.

Third. In designing any such scheme a thought must be given to inevitably varying conditions under which the building will be used. The scheme must be equally successful in full daylight and at night when brilliant window areas become large dark patches and the source of illumination is the warmer light of electricity. The interior must not depend on unobstructed sunlight and must be satisfactory both on a grey day and on a bright morning when the colour of external surroundings— the green of grass and trees or the whiteness of newly fallen snow—suffuses the interior with unaccustomed but strong reflected light.

In evolving the decorative scheme that accepts the pre-determined, every consideration must be given to the variations in the church's purposes. It will be the scene of funeral and memorial services. This at first sight implies a high degree of restraint; but reflection shows that our Faith has a constantly recurring leit-motif of hope and joy. But weddings, occasions of happiness, will also be conducted at the Holy Table. Although there is an expectation of almost a light-hearted gaiety in the decor, is it not better to remind the congregation of the solemnity of the occasion? The interior can contribute in impressing on those present memories that are rich and fragrant. Finally the many who use the church Sunday by Sunday must find peace, tranquillity and nourishment in a setting that neither palls nor bores.

So let the scheme, with unity in all its aspects, have harmony, solemn dignity, and a major dominant to which all else must be subservient.

In considering the colour scheme it will be appreciated that the medium which gives life to all is light. As architecture is modelled space, so interior decoration is captured luminosity and it is this quality that must be induced to obey intentions. Ornamentation sings its songs by virtue of light and shade; this can be fortified or muted by the use of colour. The unwanted can be suppressed and the features given appropriate accentuation by the use of colour. The hard can be dissolved and the weak strengthened by the use of colour. Under well-nigh all circumstances the intention therefore must be to capture light, and in enclosing it, teach it to provide focus, direction and memorable effects.

It is extremely unwise to lay down further general laws on a subject which is so individual in character; much depends upon conditions which are unique to each particular building. All that can be done here is to offer a few suggestions that may obviate serious errors, and to indicate types of appropriate treatment. Generally a multiplicity of colours is best avoided, since too many colours on a wall-surface tend to be distracting. The vastly differing visual (and, if an experienced organist be consulted, aural) effects of flat and glossy paint—and how with oil-bound material, both tend to yellow with time and the latter lose its high gloss—must be borne in mind. Satisfactory results may be achieved when the walls are treated so that they appear as a single colour. It is difficult to envisage any occasion when visible grading of colour—from light to dark or from one colour to another—can be aesthetically successful. In the presence of shaded surfaces—perhaps on curves and under galleries—it will be necessary to adjust the tones by trial and error so that the finished work *looks* uniform throughout. As large surfaces of wall have usually to be covered, the selection is generally best made from the greys, which may veer towards and hint at a colour, rather than applying strong and positive areas of a primary nature. This is said knowing full well that there are many occasions when there is virtue in unadulterated strength. *Pale* blues, greens and pink should be used with extreme caution. The choice and strength will be affected by the amount and quality of the light which enters the church through the windows. The old-fashioned stencilling should not be employed without unassailable reasons. White, charming in simplicity and effect, and successfully sensitive to all reflected lights, may be employed as a splendid setting for full-blooded colour in pews, hangings, good glass and a rich sanctuary treatment.

Iron pillars supporting galleries should be painted a uniform colour, with possibly the accentuation of contrast (gilding or colour) on caps and bases. The colour for columns can be a contrast to those of the general walls. For has it not been wisely said, that although construction should be decorated, decoration should not be constructed? In cases where the colour of existing pews is inconsistent, an improvement may be made by painting, bringing the wood to its natural state, bleaching or staining to a more satisfactory shade. In many churches there is a great variation in the colours of the coverings of the floor and pews. An endeavour should be made to secure uniformity or relationship in the colour of the carpets and the pew cushions. For obvious reasons seatholders should not be permitted to indulge their individual idiosyncrasies with upholstery. The woodwork throughout the church demands careful treatment which will depend on the amount of light entering the building. Gloss varnish and " graining " should be generally avoided although it is conceded that on occasions the latter may be necessary to a limited degree in the interests of matching.

Whether the proposed treatment be simple or elaborate, there are perils that are best avoided by bearing in mind wisdom born of experience.

Study the project graphically to develop ideas and gain an approximate indication of the effects to be created. Dare it be said that it is best to avoid the " free " design services offered commercially? Many paint manufacturers sell excellent materials but are not so reliable when they prepare schemes appropriate to a church.

As the decoration of a church must endure, materials of the best quality must be specified, with—and this is very important —no scamping of preparation. Supervision of the execution of the work and inspection of the sealed paint tins (top and bottom) is desirable. Flat oil paint will *always* prove to be a wiser and better investment than water-bound paints.

All colours of paint should be tried as samples *in situ* and adjusted in the light of experience under both natural and artificial illumination. This should also be carried out with all carpets, curtains and any other dominant features that may be incorporated in the scheme.

Should gilding be used—and there is no substitute for the effects it gives—it must be severely controlled in its extent. Burnished leaf which can be dulled by glazing and scumbling, and never " gold " paint, should invariably be used.

Finally: At the outset, imagination to give wings to vision will be necessary—thereafter courage. For it may well be found that many in the congregation have a prejudice, a grave and deeply rooted antipathy to colour. Such opinions must not be permitted to deflect those responsible from their intentions; in every probability the executed scheme will exercise its effects with the passage of time and all will grow, consciously or unconsciously, closer to their church and its message because of the environment. The sonorous restraint of the chords which have been brought into full harmony will sound their notes as silver trumpets, and those who use and frequent the church will be lifted. In this way, the church will be a more worthy gift to God.

In connection with the church, lettering is so frequently used that this handbook must include short notes on the very important matter. To the discerning eye nothing can be more decorative than good and characterful lettering—and nothing more revealing and distressing than bad. Much respecting the whole can be learned by the appreciative from a glance at the style (in the true sense of the word) of any lettering that may be seen.

The first criterion must be legibility. The message is intended to be read, and anything that makes this more difficult should be eliminated. To-day it is no more than a sanctimonious nineteenth century anomaly that any of the " Black " (Gothic) founts is sacrosanct. Unless there are *very* strong reasons for continuing a habit that is merely silly, the sentimentality of mock-medieval lettering should be avoided on walls, on tablets—and in print. For the earliest moveable type these letters, almost illegible to our unpractised eyes, were based on the forms derived from use of the scribe's pen. As printing became more general common-sense soon superseded these letters, with a reversion to the more easily read Roman forms which are familiar to us. In making the adaption of classic letters inscribed in stone or marble to a form that suited the exigencies of movable type certain liberties were taken. The early mechanical needs led to the adoption of letter forms which, so far as possible, all occupied an identical amount of lateral space. To take but one example, the full roundness of " O " was narrowed into an upright oval which would thus be equal in width to the naturally more slender " E " or " S ". As a direct consequence a very real debasement of fine lettering became not only common but with it the standard by which the quality of lettering was judged. But recovery came about when the improvement of mechanical techniques associated with close study of the anatomy of each letter led to many excellent new type faces which when carefully selected can now be relied upon to give character and distinction. Parallel to this scrutiny of the printed letter there is now an enhanced appreciation of those that appear in inscriptions.

The form and anatomy of every letter must speak eloquently of its function and position in the inscription. According to its neighbours, so a letter may *have* to vary. To take one example of many, " A " beside the roundness of " G " or " O " will differ from " A " following " M " or " I ". The spacing of the lettering —both between letters, between words and between lines—can be as important as the form of the individual letters. Without being unduly critical, a glance at the lettering in the average church (or for that matter over the average shop front) shows that a practice, instinctive to the Romans, is now confined to the few.

Other than in print, when all that is necessary is to select good type—it is not easy to ensure really acceptable lettering. To be spirited, lettering must be direct, show no trace of self-consciousness or affectation and be characterful. There was a time when the journeyman almost instinctively created lettering of vitality. To take two extremes it is only necessary to recall from the early nineteenth century the bold heavy Roman based letters with chunky serifs and the elegance of the flowing script, with the embellishment of flourishes, both of which figures on memorial plaques of the period. To-day such inscriptions must be designed with knowledge and executed under close super-vision. And how much our forebears can teach us about the form and design of the gravestone. . . . In addition to lettering and content theirs was the greater sensibility to the material used. Who popularised the indescriminate prevalance of un-sympathetic rock-faced or polished granite and marble?

The character and proportions of lettering will be attuned to the purpose, material and position. Forms will be modified to suit either painting, raised or incised letters, the latter of which may be coloured or gilded.

The height at which the lettering is to be placed, together with the intensity and direction of the light, will also affect the treatment and proportions.

Traditional Scottish forms of lettering can be used—in some alphabets the verticals tend to slope in an angular fashion with the words drawn close together and perhaps separated by conventional stops. Unless used with extreme care to-day, such lettering tends to the Gothick without Revival.

Much can be said in favour of the now little used tradition in our Scottish Churches that the Ten Commandments were shown inscribed on panels. There is nothing but good in this old habit which, if profitably revived, would also provide a splendid exercise in the execution of distinctive lettering.

It is not only on walls and monuments that lettering is of account. Much of the little that has been stated here on the topic of lettering has equal relevance to printing. A most earnest plea is made that congregations examine the literature that is circulated both for its information and in its name; there is no excuse whatsoever to-day for poor typography. Much bad printing within the church has its origins in thoughtless repetition from earlier days. That these characteristics are by now traditional is true enough—but, like so much else in the church these traditions date only from last century. From the pseudo-gothic alphabets to the crossed Oxford borders, all should be reviewed. Dignity coupled with legibility must become the basis for design and in following such lines we revert to earlier and infinitely preferable traditions. And it is a matter of great consequence. For it is our duty to teach and train: should we ourselves be careless and unmindful over the lesser matters, how can we expect appreciation and discrimination of the greater to flower?

MEMORIALS

THE introduction of commemorative tablets into the church creates its own problems. This is so true that it is the present fashion to discourage these wall tablets; it is therefore necessary to question whether this tendency to exclude is either wise or right. Those churches which are already crammed full must be disregarded for the moment as their probably very real problems differ. The decision that has to be made is between the clarity and simplicity of a fine uncluttered interior on the one hand and that which is regarded as being a welter of untidiness and sentiment—and possibly sentimentality—on the other. The virtues of the former and dangers of the latter are strong and self-evident.

A visit to any church with claims to age and veneration affords, through its memorials and tablets, a fascinating and revealing history of taste. How much would a little country parish church in England lose if it were stripped of its medieval tombs and brasses, should the magnificently ordered classic memorials be absent and had the elegantly inscribed plaques of the late eighteenth and early nineteenth centuries never been erected? Indeed the recently despised mid-Victorian work that is now returning to favour makes its own pronounced contribution to this unbroken tradition. And how well all these periods live together, in their somewhat random placings on the fine hallowed walls of a beloved little church. Much is to be learned of our ancestors from the very wording used on these tablets, the erection of which appeals so dearly to the best in humanity. Are we so lacking in imagination, so arrogant in mind that we set ourselves above our forebears in this? It is a tradition taken over by the Church from the pagan world which hitherto has continued without a break.

Is it the intention, in draining off all humanity, to make the church as clinically antiseptic as the operating theatre? Or is it that the church in its wisdom now can no longer find devoted sons deserving of remembrance? If the answer to these questions is in the affirmative, there is no more to be said. But if not, whatever may be our thoughts and reservations to-day, those of posterity are certain.

The few troubles that tend to cloud the matter can be rectified. From the witness of the older churches, those who designed and executed memorials in former times were in such sympathy with the prevailing intellectual climate that quality was wellnigh inevitable. To-day a similar commission could be entrusted direct to a tradesman with dire consequences. Should a memorial be installed to-day it is wise to make certain, not that it resembles any neighbours, but that in its own expressive way it reaches the same high standard. It must therefore be competently designed for the position that it is intended to occupy. Ability to design even a satisfactory memorial and give the restrained character, with its overtones of abstract qualities that is required, is rare: for much less than mastery, the power to give reasonable aesthetic expression of commemoration is not granted to all. The greatest care should therefore be taken when placing the commission. Of all works that should *not* be entrusted direct to a commercial firm, however good may be their craftsmanship, memorials come first.

The situation would be eased were congregations to establish and maintain a policy. Should the walls of the church be made available to all, then competition and crowding can follow. It should therefore be agreed that only devoted, important service and sons and daughters great in God's rather than the world's sense should be thus honoured. It assists also in achieving control and standards of distinction to bear in mind that any memorial, once accepted by the church, is extremely difficult to remove. There must be a guard against ostentation and any seeking of prestige or privilege. Limited size should be no deterrent: commemoration can be both large in concept and yet small in physical dimensions. A neat and effective general pattern can be achieved, provided only that the policy is clear.

As a memorial should surely convey a sense of endurance, it is best created out of those materials that belong to time—to withstand age, fire, wear and tear. The requisite mood which appeals to the subconscious is established with stone (rough or polished as may be appropriate), or one of the many slates or marble. The material must be carefully selected for its colour and ability to accept lettering either left as cut or emphasised with gilding or colour. Bronze, a member of the aristocracy of metals dedicated to sacred usage, has a most honourable claim. Many fine monuments have also been created from wood—the harder, such as oak, the better; this surface also accepts colour admirably. It will be observed that brass has been omitted. This is no oversight since the alloy of to-day that passes under this name is far removed from that of former days. Any of the foregoing can also be used in combination and it is always possible to insert fine enamel plaques. Usually the tablet will look better if it be set on a plate of contrasting colour and texture to separate it from the surrounding wall.

The inherent possibilities in good heraldry will not be forgotten. The armorial bearings can be in either two or three dimensions; to show tinctures it is possible to use either the conventional indications or the full pomp of blazoning. For a note on this matter and the importance of character to all lettering, reference is made elsewhere in this work.

For any tablet, such as a War Memorial, that incorporates more than a few names, great care must be exercised. It is surely best in ecclesiastical surroundings that the order should be alphabetical rather than by rank; the only exception that might be made is when the commemorated was either in, or aspired to Holy Orders. The Christian name is preferable to stark initials. In those cases of two or more names every effort must be made to verify that the one quoted on the tablet was that generally used. The completed lists should be checked and re-checked. Only those who have been responsible for such a work can know how extremely difficult it is to reach final accuracy —and the material from which the memorial has been created never lends itself to alterations, insertions and additions.

On anniversaries certain memorials may have wreaths and flowers placed beside them. Order and tidiness can be maintained if such positions are fitted as part of the design with little bronze or wrought-iron hooks.

Frequently a memorial takes the form of some fine furnishing. In these cases the record of the gift or commemoration should be kept as inconspicious as possible, and, as in all such inscriptions, have as the opening words that dedication is first and foremost " To the Glory of God ".

As a footnote to the subject (a note which refers to all work in the church) a plea is made that the names of all donors, artists, craftsmen and firms be inserted in the session minute book. All is familiar at the time, but memories are short and records all to frequently inadequate: sooner or later this information will be required.

WINDOWS

Within a church in the pale light of the north nothing can be more splendid than really good stained glass windows. As the structural possibilities of northern Gothic evolved, to make ever increasingly large windows possible, so the art of stained glass rapidly developed. It is of the north. Although understudied, this is why the medium looks and is strangely out of place in the strong light of the Mediterranean.

To achieve success, the treatment must obey well-established canons, both general and specialised; the technique has changed very little since the time of Chartres and York. There is much stained glass proposed for and in our churches which, in failing to respect these principles, is so poor in design and colour quality that it would be infinitely preferable were the window spaces filled with clear glass. The position of a stained glass window has an effect on the decoration and the quality of the light which enters the building; in colour and in treatment a window to be successful must pay certain recognition to its setting. It is not difficult to envisage a large and low cilled " east " window of such brightness during the morning, that the sanctuary or chancel, and all that is within it, is lost in the surrounding gloom. A window, although it may appear to be a fine work of art when considered in isolation, can have a disturbing effect on the general character of the church into whose walls it will be placed. It is well therefore in both old and new buildings to consult and be guided by the architect who is best versed through his training, experience and overall comprehension of all the factors and possible consequences to provide the best advice.

The relationship between new and older stained glass in a church can raise problems. It is suggested that a church whose windows are not complete should have an agreed, long-term policy. This plan, so far as possible, should embrace the interrelationship between windows, the colour sequence and a logical choice of subjects. There must be sound aesthetic advice available to those preparing the scheme. And once established and adopted, complete adherence to the plan should be enforced. To-day there is a tendency to use either clear pale colours, perhaps set in a field of white or to concentrate on gleaming jewel-like notes. Such windows, fine works in themselves, when set close to the deeper, more opaque, browner colours formerly fashionable can have a distressing effect. The difficulty may be resolved by either choosing a different position for the new window or by tempering the design and colour of the new-comer to suit its immediate neighbours. Alternatively, to the ultimate benefit of the church, the older windows may be of so poor a quality that their eventual removal and replacement can be contemplated.

It must be stressed to the utmost that a donor should not be allowed freedom of choice in selecting the position, the subject or the artist. All are important and agreement should only be reached in full consultation of the three parties concerned, the donor, the representatives of the Church (of which the minister must be the leader) and the artist. Thereafter authority must be obtained from the Presbytery and the General Trustees. Every effort must be made to encourage the appointment of an artist-craftsman, for most undistinguished results and great disappoint-ment—by the evidence of what has been done, more apparent to the sensitive eye of the discerning—are the most likely results to expect when a commercial firm is engaged. The choice of the artist is of supreme importance. He must have the ability and imagination to conceive a noble design, he must have complete mastery over his materials and he must himself select every individual piece of glass. His medium of expression is glass: the texture, the colour, the thickness and the quality each influence and affect the appearance of the completed window.

It should be obvious that satisfactory results cannot be

G

achieved when the artist's contribution ends in the design with the execution, including the choice of glass, left without his supervision to other hands. The beauty of the glass of the thirteenth and fourteenth centuries is due to the medieval craftsmen's frank use of glass and lead in simple non-naturalistic treatment of figures and pattern. There is complete and sympathetic harmony between both designer and craftsman, all having a complete understanding and mastery of the medium. The best medieval windows show a gay and splendid use of rich colours treated entirely as decoration. Where appropriate, texture and pattern is introduced. The structural leads play an important part in the outlines of the figures and other features in the composition, while the painting of details such as heads and draperies is reduced to a minimum.

What had been noble and living in the tradition ultimately fell into disuse. During the Gothic revival in the first half of the nineteenth century the art of stained glass, with certain notable, but regrettably few exceptions, was all but lost. This was followed by a period of brown and garish brightness in the latter half of the Victorian era: it is to this period that we can ascribe that multitude of windows, designed and made not as the expression of a jewel-like medium but as translucent and naturalistic pictures which disfigure so many of our churches.

Early in the present century a revival of a true understanding of the art occurred when workers in glass were no longer content to hand their designs over to others but worked themselves at bench and easel. Happily, this revival in which Scotland, with no pre-Reformation tradition, played a not undistinguished part and for which she has not yet had full recognition, has now a firm foundation. The results are to be seen in buildings ranging from Winchelsea and the Hague Peace Palace to those of our churches where there are examples of very personal work which recalls something of the thrill of the best medieval glass. Scotland can maintain this lead to-day, for she still has the artists. But survival depends on the commissions being placed.

Stained glass craftsmanship par excellence immediately recalls the glory of medieval story-telling. With everything to commend it, this is a Gothic concept which accords perfectly with the free expression of the workmanship germane to the period. This is why such windows all too frequently look strangely uncomfortable in classic interiors. If there *must* be stained glass in a church of this character, consideration should be given merely to incorporating panels of colour and decoration in broad fields of unembellished glass. Heraldry can appropriately be treated in glass: it may well be found that this is a more acceptable form for classical work, provided always that the heraldry also is classicised and not designed as mock-medieval.

When assessing a window it is important to observe the limitations imposed by the use of glass and lead. The colours must be employed for effects of expression and decoration. The lead lines of the "cames" necessary by reason of the structural part they play, along with the iron saddles set at intervals of approximately 18 inches to support the weight of the window and desirable for binding and emphasising the shapes, must be an integral part of the design. "Lights" *i.e.*, panels between jambs or mullions, over 3 feet wide will require additional vertical iron stanchion bars. Since much shading reduces the transparency of the colours, the glass should not be hidden by too heavy a coating of iron oxide which is applied on the inside to shade and treat details.

Because of the architectural setting there is need for firmness in the design of windows. It is therefore preferable that any figures should be formal rather than naturalistic, the better to harmonise with the surrounding architectural features. Severe and serene representation also lends a quality to figures, removing them from the limitations of the terrestrial element and giving them a deeper significance.

The effect of the message of a window may be great. The congregation sees it Sunday after Sunday and the influence may deeply permeate. Unlike medieval times the modern window has no didactic purpose to teach or to preach in this restricted sense; it nevertheless can quicken sensibility by bringing familiar truths to the forefront of the mind, or rouse aspirations. When the effect can be so profound, the choice of subject must be of great significance.

However elaborate the details of the window may be, the main features should make their clear and unencumbered appeal. Apart from any secondary symbolism a direct presentation should create a spiritual or ethical response. It is the combination of inspiring content and beautiful treatment that will create a full impression in the mind of the spectator. The minister and the artist must co-operate to achieve this end. The artist should be allowed to express his individual genius in the composition but he should faithfully interpret the beliefs of the Church. The treatment must be consonant in every way with the corporate beliefs of the Christian community.

A word must be said about plain glass windows. Should the so-called " cathedral glass " in rectangular or diamond panes be employed, it should be transparent and no more than delicately tinted. The days have gone when those many coloured, strongly coloured and crudely coloured areas of glass, edged with ruby or blue borders, were thought to contribute to the atmosphere of a church interior. If the outlook be, as a minimum, acceptable and not over-distracting—but preferably and more pleasantly to trees and the green fields of the countryside—it is surely better to fill the spaces with clear glass. With heating as expensive as it now is, a church with simple rectangular panes in its windows could with considerable saving insert or change to insulated glass. Each sheet is a glass box with the characteristics of a thermos flask: the depth of the check in the frame is greater than for normal glass and each panel must be fabricated to the correct sizes.

The pearly and translucent panes known as Diamond Quarries permit good passage of light. When used in leaded windows the proportions of the grid should be carefully designed, the tendency being to make the diamonds over-high for their breadth. They are probably happiest if proportioned 6 inches by 4¾ inches. The diagonal direction of the leading will be unsuited to the Georgian interior: vertical rectangles, based on one of the recognised classic principles will be more appropriate.

The place of stained glass in churches built to-day requires most careful deliberation. Should the building be one that, without being over-strongly Georgian, takes its place in the main stream of tradition, in all probability windows such as have been described will accord. But there is every likelihood that this will not be so in a building in the contemporary idiom. Against the simple calculated lines, in the absence of ornament in interiors which would be naked but for proportion, texture and chaste colour that are characteristic of so much of the best work of to-day, the familiar representational treatment of glass can both be and look extraneous. Should there be any suggestion for including such windows, the proposal is best referred to the responsible architect who is best able to advise on the correct long-term policy. While the characteristics of one design may happily accept stained glass medallions set into areas of clear glass, it may be that another is better suited to geometric or other abstract patterns. There is an interesting development of recent origin that has possibilities for ecclesiastical work. This is a treatment whereby two layers of clear glass are sealed around the edges to sandwich paper-thin fibre glass. Work ranging from broad patterns or designs in monochrome to elaborate treatment in full colour, simplified to eliminate light and shade, has been executed with great success in this medium. A further development is to set the coloured glass somewhat deeply into concrete in place of lead. This technique strongly fortifies the area of black.

There are other particularly well designed churches of to-day—often having window forms which are " nontraditional "—in which any stained glass whatsoever would be completely out of keeping and character. To force insertion under these conditions would be a serious error of judgement. There remains a golden opportunity for acquiring superb work of an individual character which, glorious in its unsullied purity, can contribute much to the totality of the church. The possibilities which are infinite lie in the working of clear glass by the hands of an artist-craftsman.

Certain techniques, some of which being by no means new, are now increasingly applied and extended to larger areas of glass. With the harmony of understanding between architect and craftsman the results can be in complete accord with architectural thought and intention of to-day. Most frequently these methods give glass that is either colourless, monochromatic, or of a single colour as a ground for a brilliantly clear and sparkling drawn design. The methods that can be applied range from sand blasting, offering varying depths, textures and subtle gradations to acid biting with a further range of effects that is controlled to obscure transparency in varying degrees. Either alone or associated with these is the further possibility of engraving and brilliant cutting, with the characteristics of a sharp, linear definition.

Actual modelling with light, which may range from the restrained to the pronounced, can be achieved through the use of cast glass into the thickness of which colour can be introduced . . . the possibilities latent in glass stimulate the imagination.

Windows have associated with them responsibilities and their problems. To permit the maximum passage of light to the interior—even clear plate-glass reduces the amount by 15 per cent—and to be seen at their best, the surfaces must be kept clean. This refers both to inside and out. It may be essential that opening panels are included for ventilation. In recognising the presence of such elements, the architect will accept their presence within the general lines of his design. The method of control can be important; cords can look unsightly and break, poles used carelessly shatter valuable glass and mechanical gears are clumsy as they snake their way from transom down to operating crank. Possibly the neatest solution is to have the openings in side lights fixed on horizontal centre pivots. Two simply renewed operating wires, the one to open and the other to close, can then be threaded through tubes concealed in the walls to travel down to a level convenient for operation.

For particularly valuable glass, outside protection will be necessary. This can take the form of galvanised wire mesh which, in association with light glass or under strong lighting conditions, can be visible internally. Alternatively, further clear glazing can be added on the outside. On the assumption that the void between the two glass layers can be kept clean, it may be thought that this expedient should also have thermal and sound insulating properties. Unfortunately efficiency worthy of consideration for the former requires hermetic conditions, and for the latter a distance of some 9 inches between the two panes of glass.

Most church windows, being large, will have their condensation problems. Brought about by the warm internal air, with its higher water content coming into contact with the glass cooled by external temperatures, the surplus moisture is deposited on the colder surfaces. The effects can be mitigated by the formation of little cill line gutters formed close to the glass and drained through small bore pipes which, led through the wall thickness to discharge outside, must be kept clear and clean if they are to operate.

PICTURES, PAINTINGS AND MOSAICS

CLAIMS have been put forward that the Church of Scotland should use mosaic and painting as mural decoration in their own rights. No one of any degree of knowledge will contest that both media are capable of the most superlative decorative effects, and that wherever practicable and sensible their use should be encouraged to the utmost. There is nothing new in finding the Church acting as a patron of the Arts and in consequence gaining more than she gives. This relationship declined over recent centuries to the Church's loss but is now regaining ground through the actions of men of vision. An important consideration—as ever—is the calibre of the artist to be entrusted with the project. And there must be certainty beyond question that the setting is appropriate.

Mosaic decoration—stone or encaustic tesserae for the floor, with the additional choice of glass for the walls—demands isolation: so powerful, so rich, so wonderful are the effects that there is a very real danger of detriment to less telling features. Also the lighting must be most carefully considered.

With precisely similar considerations, mural painting brings with it a further important point. The painted, frescoed or tempera surfaces should be as large as circumstances warrant. The history of Art shows that ability to cover huge areas is well within human power and has led to the most tremendous results. Following a period of neglect this art is now reviving and attracting greater interest. The Church can benefit itself and perform an important service of art to the public by giving every possible encouragement in all cases that are justified by circumstances. To-day our more active tradition favours easel canvasses and some may doubt whether our artists, with notable exceptions, are generally at ease and successful when confronted with almost limitless space. The validity of this doubt has not been proved.

It is possible also to include " framed " pictures. Without extreme care they will occur rather as incidental furnishings and lack the majesty and architectonic qualities of mural decoration. A guard must be made against anything that resembles an altarpiece. Broadly speaking such a painting will appear more effective and take its place the better in its architectural setting where the treatment is in areas of colour rather than where the emphasis is on atmospheric statement. It must be emphasised that the setting is of great importance. The canvas or panel should not be hung in a haphazard way on the wall, but be made to fit in with its architectural background. For example it can be set flush on the wall, in a good light, and surrounded by a simple wood moulding, or be incorporated in some form of panelling. Such pictures painted in the normal technique of oil paint on canvas or to a lesser extent on wood panels are highly susceptible to changes in temperature and humidity, to currents of air and to direct sunlight. Pictures hung against a stone wall should be insulated with an air space by having the backs slightly clear of the wall surface behind. Similarly rear ventilation should be provided for any pictures set into panelling so that conditions on the front and at the back are identical.

Artificial illumination may be thought to be necessary for the paintings. Where circumstances make this necessary, there are two points to bear in mind. First: normal " picture " lights— a hooded top light—even when thrown well forward produce a patch of brilliance that all too soon fades into lower darkness. The correct treatment is to project the light from some distance in such a way that the edges of the illumination are masked to accord exactly with the shape of the picture. And second: the normal artificial light being considerably warmer than daylight will affect the colour, balance and values of the painting. How-ever attractive it may look under this condition, it is not seen as the painter intended. It follows that wherever possible a cooler, more natural light should be utilised.

Either mosaic, mural or painting will be unhappy in the presence of stained glass—unless the latter be confined to formal and unassertive patterns or quite small and incidental features.

HALLS

To say the least of it, it is odd that church halls—and hall-churches—are frequently planned around the physical dimensions of a double badminton court. Be this as it may, it is this area which appears conveniently to provide space for the requisite number of chairs when seated as an auditorium.

The planning of a successful hall is not simple, being dependent on a full comprehension of the differing purposes to be served. A large part of the skill will show itself in the manner in which space, governed by economy, is grouped so that rooms are multi-purpose. Failure with the basic layout, flexibility and inter-relationships can only result in a serious curtailment of the smooth running of the work of the congregation.

Entrances. The hall must have outside access, at which vehicles can draw up. This, being dependent on design and economy, may or may not be independent of the main entrance to the church. Where separate, the hall suite will nevertheless require to be linked to the church. There should be vestibule space, perhaps shared with other ancillary accommodation, to act as a crush hall, a draught trap that contains the warmth within the hall and which can provide generous space for hats and coats. Linked with the vestibule, it is desirable to have lavatories for both sexes. Direct exit under crowd conditions must also be considered.

The Kitchen. The Achilles' Heel frequently lies in the kitchen with which the hall will be associated. Thought directed towards effective and efficient planning here will add vastly to the success of the whole, bearing in mind that the staff will be amateur—and rightly critical. The kitchen is best planned to localise those all-pervading smells and should be separated from the hall by " In " and " Out " doors giving access to a service space. This can be fronted by a long table or counter—which can be de-mountable—possibly incorporating a hot-plate. Obviously it must be possible to by-pass this barrier. For laying out cups and washing up in the kitchen there must be plentiful bench-top space. Although bakers' trays vary considerably in size, racks into which they may be slid will prove convenient. Side by side there should be two sinks, the one to wash and the other to rinse, with a plentiful and instantaneous supply of hot water. These sinks, with generous draining boards laid to fall on either side do not need to be beneath windows, for the view is of no importance when washing up: but a good concentration of natural and artificial light (with carefully positioned taps) is desirable to minimise breakages. No establishment that is concerned with food preparation can claim to be up to date if it does not include a washhand basin.

No more than limited cooking facilities will be required. The likely demands will be for the preparation of tea and coffee in considerable bulk and the ability to heat and keep hot light foodstuffs. The solution may lie in the inclusion of a normal domestic cooker augmented with a boiling hot-plate. An electric extract fan or, preferably, a full canopy will do much to assist both comfort and the life of decoration. The economics of the alternative fuels and the wishes of users must be carefully studied.

The kitchen should be generously supplied with fitted cupboards, one of which may be a ventilated larder. Fitted with a sink, the cleaner's closet for the entire building may be planned within this area where hot water is readily available, and should be large enough, with adequate shelving, to hold all the cleaning equipment—buckets, brooms, brushes and the vacuum cleaner. It is helpful to the ladies who will work in the kitchen if provision is made for limited cloak space, and a w.c. A service access should be so placed that, without blocking other entrances, delivery vans can back in.

So far as concerns treatment and finish, the kitchen floor should be impervious and resilient. In place of tiling which is now deemed hygienically unsatisfactory (because of the joints) walls are best oil painted or enamelled to permit washing down. An eye must be kept, particularly with regard to the ceiling, on minimising condensation. Certain working surfaces may be scrubbed; all other woodwork should be protected with paint, varnish or plastic covering. The specification for bench tops is important: such surfaces should have an upstanding wall skirting and be fitted with an edge lip projecting slightly above the top. On the supposition that all cutting will be done on boards, linoleum is possibly the optimum covering for top surfaces being semi-soft, colourful, scrubbable and easily maintained. It may be noted in passing that sheet plastic material should be avoided for this particular purpose since wet crockery placed on such a surface develops an uncanny facility to creep. The kitchen premises should be bright, cheerful and well ventilated. Inevitably they will be noisy. To counteract this as far as possible, the most should be made of any absorbent that can be introduced: a few chairs with washable cushions, curtains, an occasional rug and possibly an acoustic ceiling.

The Stage. The platform will be required for purposes as diverse as the opening of sales of work, lectures, and addresses, concerts and dramatic performances. With a lively and vital congregation it may be that some Sunday School classes will find no alternative but to use this area as an overflow space.

The usefulness of the stage is heavily handicapped if there is neither proscenium (with adequate side space) to take curtains nor back-stage access to changing accommodation. That such rooms on a level with the platform may also serve other purposes is of no moment: a large Sunday School room, useful also for small classes and choir practices, which is divisible by folding partitions or in extreme instances curtains will serve. There should be access to lavatories for both sexes.

While there is no intention that the stage should be over-large or over-lavish it is essential that a cast should be able to pass from one side to the other without being seen. Possibly the full depth, only required occasionally, can best be obtained through the addition of a demountable apron. The stage itself must be resilient: if not carried on timber joists, the essential boarded finish should rest on wood fillets firmly fixed to the substructure. The floor is best flat and not raked, and its height above the floor level of the hall determined by a study of sight lines. Almost inevitably the platform will turn out to be surprisingly high. A chair store with direct and easy access—which certainly will be used for keeping much more than the hall seating and cannot therefore be over generous—will be demanded. This can be tucked beneath the stage.

Reasonable and flexible lighting facilities will be required. The stage is best fitted with domestic lighting for all normal purposes which can be removed on theatrical occasions to be replaced by overhead battens, footlights, with floods and spots fitted in the hall itself. All lighting must be controlled from back-stage—including " house " fittings which will thus be at least two way. It is helpful if a square fitted projection screen can be included towards the front of the stage. Doubtless wiring should be incorporated for the use of microphones and the reproduction of sound tracks through loudspeaker amplifiers.

Access to the stage and supporting accommodation requires thought. From the floor of the auditorium up to the platform may be best effected for all normal purposes by portable but steady stepping—provided there is an alternative doored route elsewhere. The stage and other accommodation, which must have direct escape to the open air, will not be placed on the wall that contains the entrances for the audience.

While provision will be made overhead for hoisting and fixing scenery, under normal conditions the stage should look and be a " finished " recessed portion of the hall. Such decorative emphasis and treatment that may be appropriate should accord with the scheme for the whole.

The foregoing remarks concerning the layout of backstage accommodation should be taken as being for general guidance only. In all cases where serious dramatic enthusiasm is likely it would be well to consult either an experienced amateur group or theatre before plans are finalised.

The Hall. As has been implied, the most probable shape will be rectangular with a flat floor. And the basic requirements will be obvious. It must be well lit, the placing of doors must accord with its several uses, the acoustic properties must give reasonable reverberation without too much drumming and echo, and it must be wired for convenient switching and projection. Having to serve such varied purposes, some of which may tend to the rough, the choice for finish and decorative treatment together with the benefits of a protective dado must be assessed. It will be necessary to study and possibly suggest how the Sunday School can best operate. Many teachers like to be able to separate their charges into small groups; a hall dado treatment that pulls out to 90° to form divided bays is useful for segregation. It will be appreciated that the smaller the ages of the children so the greater the floor space required. With a floor that as often as not will be clear of seating it will be difficult to have each chair fixed or fixible in its correct position. Chairs should therefore be battened or clipped together in numbers convenient to handle, with at least the front and back rows positioned and end fixed to the floor surface with countersunk removable bolts. Normally no chair should be more than six places away from a gangway: seven will therefore be permitted at the sides, with thirteen for centre blocks. The front to back spacing of chairs should be as generous as possible to provide knee and passing space, nothing less than 2 feet 6 inches being acceptable. The choice of chairs is also important. The selection is best made from those which are stackable. Canvas seats tend to sag with a little time and use and thus become very much more fatiguing than shaped plywood or formed plastic. As with so much else, the cheapest may prove expensive.

Curtains, lined for durability, drape and density, with or without blinds for black-out purposes, will be required for privacy and projection: the introduction of such fabrics offers acoustic improvement and splendid decorative possibility. The material selected will be chosen with laundering in mind. When considering the form and nature of the windows the question of ventilation will arise. In view of the fact that the windows will so frequently be closely curtained when the hall is in full use, any opening lights will best be augmented by further manually controlled ventilation grilles in the walls, ceiling or both.

Because of the number of people that will use the hall, the overall length and breadth will necessitate a reasonable height to obviate any feeling of depression. To avoid over many lighting points, it will be necessary that the level be raised and the power of light fittings increase to provide adequate illumination over the entire floor area. Provided that the hall roof construction does not have low trusses, this arrangement should admirably suit badminton.

IT is important that the congregation should not only see but also hear equally well. As is said elsewhere in this handbook the two are inter-dependent in so far as those with unobstructed vision tend to have their interest and concentration held—and they listen. These conditions obviously apply to the relationship of the entire congregation with the Communion Table, the pulpit and the lectern. Music within the church is, or should be, of great importance. But acoustic conditions for music differ from those that best serve speech. In these circumstances a degree of compromise and sacrifice is necessary, since the hearing of the voice must have precedence. This section is therefore devoted entirely towards the voice, the conditions for music being broadly described under " Organs and Choirs ". Needless to say these remarks have no reference to deaf aids, the installation of which, where called for, is straightforward electrical engineering.

In any new church full consideration will be given to these functional necessities and little, if any, physical efficiency need be sacrificed for architectural effect and atmosphere. Through careful design in the placing and treatment of doors and windows, the layout and finish of vestibules and planning to have the occupied areas within columns, and avoiding side aisle seating, the effects of extraneous noises from traffic on surrounding streets can be greatly reduced. Thereafter the question of acoustics becomes dependent on volume, shape, height, areas for reflection and absorption—all matters best left to the expert. In new buildings these are subjects in all their details for the competence of the architect, and, being of a highly technical nature, lie outwith the scope of this work.

Existing churches that are not satisfactory for audition can

H

often be improved. In buildings which are unduly lofty, large or " hard ", hearing conditions are frequently bad in spite of good sight lines; too often rectification is sought through the agency of microphones, amplifiers and speakers. On occasions such mechanical aids do assist, and are indeed necessary, but a very careful diagnosis of the trouble should most certainly be made before resorting to electrical appliances as the panacea. Frequently in " difficult " churches the introduction of an even greater volume of sound is the worst possible step to take.

Initially it is obviously important to verify that the minister is using his voice correctly for the building in which he speaks. This is not so simple as it appears at first sight, for to-day many speakers are instinctively microphone conscious. Where there is no amplifying system the pitch, speed and direction of delivery must be modulated and regulated to suit the building. Where the microphone is used, the converse becomes true: the speaker must control his voice almost at conversational level so that he relies on the individual amplifiers to spread his voice as necessary. Failure to co-operate with the mechanical system results in confusion, harshness and distortion.

The churches that are acoustically troublesome tend to exemplify some or all of the following characteristics:—

(i) They have what is known as a long reverberation period, which is most likely to occur in lofty buildings. This is to say that any one sound or note takes an appreciable and measurable time to die down to inaudibility.

(ii) The surfaces are " hard "—stone, plaster, large areas of glass or other non-absorbent materials.

(iii) The church markedly improves for the ease of preaching and hearing as it is more nearly full. This is directly associated with (i) and (ii) since people themselves act as absorbents. The condition can be tested simply by a clap of the hands or a staccato note on the organ. Should inaudibility take longer than two seconds when the church is two-thirds full, it can be concluded that conditions are less satisfactory than they might be.

(iv) Trouble of a different technical nature may be experienced where there is a semi-circular apse, domes or a shaped ceiling overhead. The explanation in this case is that the church is experiencing a particular and unfortunate condition of echo; improvement lies in damping the blurred jangle at its source by the introduction of absorbents and not in adding to the condition through the introduction of mechanical agents.

In semi-scientific language, sound waves take measurable time to travel; on meeting a hard surface they behave as does light on a mirror or a ball bounced against a wall. They are reflected back at an angle equal to the angle of incidence. It will be appreciated that any listener who is in an unobstructed position hears the waves direct and at the distance he is from the speaker. But he *also* is subjected to sound waves which, reflected back to him from ceilings, rear walls and all other " hard " surfaces and thus having further to travel, are delayed in reaching him. Should the difference in time between these waves be too great then the " edge " of the sound becomes blurred. In terms of distance a difference of 60 feet between the direct and reflected sound waves can be regarded as being the maximum. In other words, a listener sitting 20 feet away from the speaker under a 40 foot high reflecting ceiling is verging on a critical position since the path of the reflected wave is the sum of its travel upwards and thereafter downwards. As these variations in length and time increase, so the definition of speech becomes less clear; it is thus that any church with these characteristics gains the reputation of being one in which hearing is difficult.

Where such conditions occur acutely enough as to be

troublesome, rectification lies in the replacement of the offending reflecting surfaces by absorbents. Such surfaces will generally be found to be walls facing the speaker, high ceilings and, as noted above, shaped surfaces. Absorbents for introduction can take many forms, ranging from acoustic tiles and special plaster, to curtains, upholstery and carpets. It is frequently a simple matter to experiment by generously draping the rear wall and elsewhere with blankets and curtains to find out empirically whether conditions better themselves. Should this be the case (as is likely) treatment then becomes a matter of degree. Draping the rear wall with heavy and lined curtains will help, but should this be undesirable visually, the surfaces can be covered with acoustic plaster, or sheathed with perforated biscuit-like tiles or strips. It should be observed that care must be taken when re-decorating these materials. Spray painting only should be permitted since brush application can build up a pore-filling film or skin which will entirely defeat the functioning of the absorbents. Hard pews can be heavily cushioned and aisles covered with thick carpeting, both of which will assist.

It is perhaps worth noting that in certain surroundings existing elaborate suspended light fittings may be assisting to disrupt unwanted sound waves. They should only be removed—say, in modernising the interior—with care, else their absence may be seriously felt. In older buildings the presence of modelled enrichment and decoration—and the films of dust that it gathers—acts as a splendid absorbent. The removal of such features, in the interests of bringing the interior more into line with to-day's taste, can become dangerous from the acoustic point of view.

In more extreme cases, overhead treatment should also be contemplated, substituting a flat absorbent surface at a lower level for any high and possibly curved or shaped ceiling.

In reducing the unwanted reflected sound waves it will be well to check that all reasonable precautions are taken to reinforce those that are direct. A " hard " wall behind the Communion

Table will help. This should be smooth and polished and can be stone, wood panelling, hard plaster or a window. The lectern and pulpit are improved by a similar reflecting background. A sounding board overhead, which as we know can provide a splendid opportunity as a decorative feature, can also assist. It is important that the reflecting surface, which can be shaped to direct the sound to the more distant seats, should exceed the area of the pulpit considerably. In churches with deep galleries directional reflectors can be fitted to the undersides to augment the sound waves reaching the rearmost seats. It must be realised that these suggestions serve to direct and reinforce the output of sound; by their nature they can do nothing to create more sound; nor do they bend the waves round columns and corners to seats that are hidden.

Apses, domes and shaped ceilings have been mentioned. In such cases acoustic effects will be of a slightly different nature. The laws governing the behaviour of sound being consistent, there is every likelihood that the reflected waves will be focussed to converge on certain points or small areas, and thus produce a feeling of discomfort ranging from slight to acute for those sitting in the vicinity. Rectification lies in identifying and treating the offending reflecting surfaces with the most efficient absorbent material.

Implicit in all that has been said is the understanding that any steps taken produce visually acceptable results. While curtains should be heavy and decorative, new plaster can, where appropriate, be treated as a field for colour, pattern and perhaps symbolism and painting.

The foregoing has been written to give a degree of comprehension on the causes and possible treatment of acoustic problems. But any church contemplating extensive rectification is strongly recommended to place itself in skilled professional hands.

The extremely large and long basilican church, or those with many columns and aisles, will probably best be served by an amplifying system which can carry sound the full length and around corners in a way that is otherwise impossible. This is not to say that such churches may not also require the introduction of absorbents. In every probability steps must also be taken to see that the more rapidly carried reproduced sounds do not blur the more slow moving natural waves.

The technique of such an installation is complex, every case being an individual problem. This is far beyond the scope or intention of this handbook, and expert, professional rather than commercial, advice should invariably be sought.

In every probability the technicalities of heating systems will be of but passing interest, the detailed information on such matters being, in any case, outwith the scope of this work. Nevertheless this short section outlining basic principles is included as it may simplify both a consultant's explanation and a hearer's understanding of possibilities.

In the instance of a new church, the architect will have his own views stemming from many aspects of his work. He may have with him his professional and specialist adviser. It is with them that the entire matter should be discussed. An existing church that wishes to install a new system or modernise an existing outmoded plant may not have a disinterested mind so readily available and yet prior decision on certain fundamental matters is desirable. A commercial representative who gains a hearing will undoubtedly represent his employers interests.

Flexibility of control is essential. No congregation wishes to pay for heating the entire extent of the premises when only a part is to be used. The installation should therefore be designed in sensible circuits, the hall, the ancillary accommodation and the church proper at least being each independent of the others.

Heating can be expensive to operate and no congregation wishes to dissipate its funds on warming the outside of its building. It follows that wherever possible good insulation to keep warmth in and cold out (with the reverse in summer) is more than an economy: it is a common sense and essential expenditure. The roof space is usually the greatest source of leakage but walls also can be treated to conserve warmth.

One of the problems with the heating of church buildings lies in intermittent use. The premises tend to be used more often in the evenings, with the church itself frequently at week-ends only. To be comfortable, the building must be warmed well in advance of use, after which additional heat will be largely wasted. This intermittent pattern of rising and falling temperatures is a further reason for stressing the importance of insulation.

Draughts are the bane of many a church—the subject looms so large as to approach warranting a section devoted to it. In planning a building to-day control will be considered: in an older building their reduction can be assisted by a well-designed heating system. Churches tend to be high buildings, and warmth created at the floor rises. In so doing the cold air at the higher level, being displaced, is thus forced downwards—and is called a draught. That the warm air which has risen may be prematurely cooled by a poorly insulated roof construction and clerestorey windows merely accelerates this movement of air. The correct technique, which is no false economy, is deliberately to heat the upper reaches of the building to a temperature sufficiently high as to prevent the "wanted" warmed air from rising too rapidly.

The layout of every piped system and those which depend on visible heating elements require careful consideration. Pipe runs must be positioned in such a way that they cause the minimum inconvenience. It is important to realise that a gravity-fed installation depends on the heated water circulating: at the outset the hot water rises from the boiler to the highest point of the system and, as the temperature falls, finds its way back to the starting point by cooling and by being pressed onwards by further rising hot water. On reaching the boiler it is re-heated and re-circulated. Under these circumstances it will be appreciated that loops, particularly upwards, perhaps to encircle doors, become obstructions. The system must *fall*. It follows that the design of the pipe runs must be carefully arranged not only to function efficiently, but to be economic and tidy. Into such consideration must be taken the fact that warmed air rises from the hot surfaces and, with the air movement, particles of dust which are deposited along walls—particularly at the points to which the pipes are held by metal fixings. The circuit should therefore also be designed, so far as possible, not to affect decoration. The reason for deflecting " shelves " with little downward sides and caulked tightly at the back above those radiators which abutt against walls is obvious. As there is no purpose in warming walls, there is sense also in placing insulated panels behind such radiators.

One traditional method for removing the problems of pipe runs is to have the circuit contained in sub-floor ducts with the warm air rising through pierced metal floor grilles. Being difficult to clean, or neglected because not obvious, such ducts harbour dirt and dust, much of which is carried up with the rising warmed air.

The placing of the radiators will obviously be scrutinised. They must not occur where, under any circumstances, they could be inconvenient. For example they should not be located so that they inhibit any re-arrangement of seating. It is also important that all lobbies, vestibules and entrance halls are heated at least to the temperature of the church itself. This is not a humanitarian suggestion made for the comfort of those who will be on duty in such places; it is to assist in minimising air movement within the church.

For all systems operating on heated water, solid fuel remains the most economic to buy; each congregation must decide whether it is the cheapest to burn. For such fuel implies time, even with the refinement of automatic stokers—time to heat up after kindling, time to stoke and time to dispose of ash. And time is an expensive commodity.

Some aspects of the foregoing are ameliorated by fuelling the central boiler with the more expensive gas or oil. In the latter instance the storage tanks should be large enough to give the advantages of bulk buying. Contingent on availability of fuels, comparisons on running costs should be obtained since there may be no great disparity between the costs. It is advisable to provide for convertable burners in the boiler to guard against any future non-availability of fuels.

The choice to be made lies between low and high tempera tures and between gravity operated and pumped systems. The danger element of burning from contact with steam pipes is avoided with low pressure hot water, but normally pipe bores and radiator surfaces require to be larger. The gravity system is the simplest to operate, but the negotiation of doors, aisles and changes in level may make the introduction of a pump essential. Should the decision be to warm through the agency of water, all aspects should be discussed with the designer entrusted with the preparation of the scheme. The factors that must be examined are the capital costs of the installation, includ-ing the building of the heating chamber, and the running costs in terms of fuel, time and maintenance.

It is assumed that a major warmed air ventilation plant operating through ducts will be beyond the scope of the average congregation. But the potentialities of electricity as the heating medium must be examined. An electrically operated boiler will probably be rejected in that more costly fuel will be consumed in a system whose capital cost will show no real reduction.

Electricity can be used locally with profit. Local oil-filled radiators operated thermostatically offer one solution. While Night Store heaters are a further possibility, it will be realised that they are what the name implies: material in considerable bulk which is heated at off-peak hours to transmit its temperature to the surrounding air over a period of time. With many advantages, the chief detraction is a lack of flexibility on the occasions of sudden calls—greatest output of heat in the morning when greatest demand is possibly in afternoons and evenings when the full advantages of the " off-peak " rates are lost. Analogous in theory is underfloor heating where the bulk of material to be heated is the structure of the floor itself. This is most easily installed in a new building that can be provided with a concrete structural floor fully insulated against loss of heat by downward and edge transmission. The choice of floor finishes that can be laid on top present no serious problems: with hardwoods care in choice must be exercised but otherwise the sole requirement is contact with the heated mass below.

An existing floor of traditional construction may well be unsuitable or uneconomic to adapt for floor heating. At first sight apparently more expensive to run than systems operated from a boiler, a more searching analysis should be made before the final decision is reached regarding any electrical installation. The capital costs of installation will be so much reduced that the resulting figures cannot be disregarded. The dirtiness of the more traditional systems is avoided, in consequence of which a considerable increase to the life of decoration can be anticipated. And all this is obtained in obedience to a switch which in itself can be automatic.

ILLUMINATION

In an old and perhaps historic church the installation of a lighting scheme that is both sympathetic and efficient is not an easy matter; no congregation should embark on any such project without the fullest and best possible advice. Full recognition is given here for the helpful services that are provided by the commercial manufacturing concerns. It must be realised however that generally it is their business to provide their concept of the requisite illumination at the points where such lighting is required and, in spite of the assurances that will be given, not necessarily to enhance the atmosphere and architectural qualities of the building. So far as concerns the professional electrical engineer, his knowledge, his expertise is essential; but he is not trained aesthetically and will be the first to seek such assistance. If he does not, he is best avoided. It is advisable therefore to consult a sensitive architect on the understanding that he will work in the closest liaison with a professional illumination engineer.

The problems of the more average church building, be it new or old, are similar, but perhaps simpler to solve. The requisite intensity of light is easily determined by meter, calculation or reference; how to turn the result into reality is more complex. Many a treatment that is in normal use, at best of moderate functional success and no enhancement to the interior, is frequently commissioned because it is cheap (which it looks), "efficient" (which is questionable) and easily serviced (as considered by those who do not have to undertake re-lamping). Frequently the best installation can be one which throws light forward from behind the congregation. In these instances it must be remembered that the church will be seen in *both* directions and every effort must be made to ensure seemliness from all points of view. Commercial tube fittings or spot lights concealed on one side only by roof trusses or wall breaks are no true solution. Little better is a ceiling liberally sprinkled with bull's eye portholes often criss-crossed with a pattern of safety wires. Leaving aside the undesirable flattening effects that such clinical illumination has on all internal architectural modelling, the disruption to the plane of the ceiling and the inference that, glare or no glare, no one is meant to glance upwards, tend to make this form of lighting undesirable. It can kill character.

Special regard must be paid to the effects of the internal lighting on any large areas of stained glass at night. Such glazing can then become no more than a large and dreary pool of unbroken leadlike darkness. Whenever possible the interior lighting should be arranged to play its part in creating articulation and sparkle on all such windows to give a degree of relief and interest.

As with all else, the basis of any successful solution will arise from a clear understanding of the nature of the problem. The object is simply to throw a predetermined intensity of light as equally as possible over an area of seating. It is important to remember that, first, glare to other seats must be avoided, and second, in the interests of economy, that the intensity of light is governed by the distance of the throw. As the dimension between the light and the lit increases, so the intensity of illumination is reduced on a geometric progression. If light is of a given intensity at 10 feet from the source, this will be reduced to one-quarter at 20 feet.

It will be appreciated that any system of lighting depends on a happy and reasonable balance. It is difficult to generalise as interiors can vary so much in lightness and darkness, the one requiring less and the other more artificial light. Character must also be taken into account. A delicate Georgian church will require much greater light and lightness—possibly with upward supplementary light—than will be appropriate for a vaulted or

darkly trussed interior. While circumstances will determine
the degree of illumination necessary for each case, 10 foot
candles can be accepted as being a reasonable level. To have the
light bulbs close to the plane to be illuminated—the height of a
service book held standing—would result in an unreasonably
large number of fittings over the entire area of the church.
Therefore the sources of light must be reduced in number and
lifted to give a satisfactory pattern of fittings with the intensity
stepped up correspondingly.

It will be found that indirect lighting—that is to say lighting
from totally concealed sources shining up to the ceiling to be
reflected downwards—is seldom satisfactory and has a high
consumption of current. In itself it tends to have a depressing
effect. It also has the disadvantage that the upward beams can
cast shadows in the direction opposite to those intended by
nature and designed by man.

Satisfactory appearances are contingent on good, intelligent
design. Any feature that lends itself to the introduction of
rhythm, repetition and enhancement of the sense of perspective
within the church must be welcomed: this is precisely the effect
that can be expected with suspended light fittings. These should
be kept to either side rather than be placed centrally. It is only
necessary to reflect on some familiar monument to realise how
much is contributed by the slow steady march of repeated
fittings, each hanging on a suspension whose termination is
lost overhead; subsidiary echoes of gleaming metal, further
notes of interest that provide scale, in the form of small decorative elements, can be introduced at intervals on the length of the
chains.

While theoretical success can lie with light fittings, the
practical application is no simple matter. Our forefathers had
no doubts as to their problem and its solution. The glazing of
the Renaissance lanterns, splendidly carved and gilded on scarlet
posts which permitted processional use, screened the flame from

draught and danger; the many branched candle fittings of
bronze or brass, easily lowered for attention, glowed hand-
somely in sixteenth century interiors; and the cataracts of
crystal of diamond brilliance accorded perfectly with the lightness of the Rococo. We have not yet achieved an equivalent
success. To acquire antique fittings and " modernise " them to
take electrically operated candles is no solution. As a gesture
such " candles " are without meaning, as illumination ineffective
and as a deceit unsuccessful. Should old fittings, most of which
are lovely in themselves, be available, they should be converted
so that they look like and function as part of an electrical
installation.

For the interior that passes under the stylistic label of " contemporary ", the choice of attractive, suitable and reasonably
priced stock articles is embarrassingly large; the only difficulties
that need be anticipated lie in decision and the possibility of
seeing identical fittings elsewhere. With a more traditional
building the choice is not so easy, for in this case trade catalogues
tend to be unhelpful. Perhaps it is needless to caution against
the bulk of those designs which have been given a so-called
ecclesiastical flavour.

It is not only possible but rewarding and exhilarating to
design purpose-made decorative and functionally efficient light
fittings. When of true craftsmanship and correctly placed these
can and do add a superb note to the ensemble. When such
fittings are elaborate they are dependent for effect and efficiency
on cleverly contrived reflectors, beautiful glass or lavishly worked
bronze or gilded wrought-iron to mention a few possibilities.
They can represent much thought and time spent on design and
execution. In consequence they can be expensive. There will be
many churches which, however great may be ambition, must
find a more economic solution. In such cases the approach
should be through restraint associated with logic and knowledge.

At the outset ascertain the necessary degree of illumination which in turn will indicate the number of points at a predetermined height. Then select a stock diffuser or shade—or one that is simply made—which will direct the light where needed and obviate glare from all normal viewpoints. It will be appreciated that architectural effect can be found through the careful handling of a repeat motif; such elements, grouped in straight lines, circles, stars, crosses or tiered crowns, should float in a rhythmic pattern over the illuminated area. The lighting points may rest on, be suspended closely to, or some distance from their supporting framework. The nature of this carriage will be determined by the desired shape and spread of the fitting. Subject to the general dictates of design, the material can be polished or painted timber; further possibilities lie in the use of tubes or wrought or cast metal left, according to the choice, in a natural condition or gilded, painted, lacquered or enamelled. The key to success lies in the realisation that the effect is gained by repetition of lights and that the support is intended to do no more than the word implies: unless a particular character is sought the carriage should be as slender and inconspicuous as possible and the design such that a skilled local craftsman can be entrusted with the work in every confidence that he will make a positive contribution.

The area that contains the Holy Table will require even more particular care: in this part of the building the intensity and warmth of the light can be increased. But true of all else in the church every effort must be made to exercise restraint, to guard against both the theatrical and, worst of all, the sentimental. By all means flood light on to the Cross, but do not under any circumstances have it illuminated from within.

Consideration should be given to servicing. Obviously all light fittings should be kept clean and bright if they are to function at their best. This can imply that glassware, smooth on inside and out, is easier to maintain than are faceted surfaces.

Wherever possible fittings should be easily accessible for the attention that they will inevitably require. It may be of interest to note that bulbs placed horizontally have their lives considerably reduced. The anticipated life of lamps being predictable, should fixed fittings be so high that tall steps or trestles become necessary, thought should be given to a contract with an electrician for a complete relamping at determined intervals.

Consideration will naturally be given to the switching arrangements, with the board positioned so that control can be exercised conveniently. The scuffle of feet and the subsequent staccato of switches can be disturbing to a congregation. In consequence, as the lighting is frequently lowered during the sermon the gear is best sited outside (but perhaps cupboarded) in the vestibule. A refinement which adds to comfort and prolongs the life of bulbs is to introduce dimmers. It is only sensible to carry spare fuses—not merely fuse wire—convenient to insert in the case of an emergency.

Elsewhere the more obvious problems associated with local lighting have been mentioned under the appropriate headings. The remainder, of which there are many, ranging from points for the Christmas tree to the lectern, from the vestibule to the vestry can be decided each on its own merits. It will be well to see that temporary additions that may be made for any purpose do not overload their circuits.

Where a new installation is under consideration the advantages in economy, flexibility and simplicity that are to be gained through the introduction of a ring main should be assessed. This technical matter should be discussed with an electrical expert, bearing in mind that it is not every tradesman who is anxious to recommend a system that materially reduces the work on which he bases his charges.

In general, it will be important that the colour of light to be introduced is considered in relationship to the colour scheme of the church. Unless for special effects and occasions, colours other

I

than those known by such terms as " Natural " or " Daylight " can be regarded as suspect.

All churches will also be interested in external lighting to illuminate paths, steps and doorways. A few may consider floodlighting. Should there be any likelihood of this being used frequently, then thought should be given to the advisability of making at least the wiring permanent. By lighting in this way possibly stained glass windows (but only if they be good), a fine tower or an open bell a new and unexpected interest can be added to the church.

BIBLIOGRAPHY

SHOULD there be lessons in this handbook, they are twofold.

The first surely is that true achievement in creative work derives from an acceptance, either consciously or unconsciously, of the dictum that Form follows Function. To reach a fuller understanding of the subject matter it is therefore suggested that study be given to the origins, development and aims of the Church of Scotland. With the enlarged comprehension that the works given in the first list below will provide, greater and more apt significance can certainly follow.

The second is that Truth should express itself at all times. What is Truth? The very word, representing an abstract quality, evades precise definition. In the context of the Visual Arts it remains an essential attribute that, with training and experience, can usually be recognised. When it is said that Truth is Beauty and Beauty, Truth the statement can only be accepted with the provision that there is certainty of interpretation. For Beauty, a dangerous word which the text of this book does not stress, reveals itself mysteriously as an all important by-product. It is the jewel found in the foot of the crucible when gifted men, artists in the media of their work, have reached significant solutions to their problems. Recognition and appreciation of this Force, which ranges from the simplicity of the child or flower to the majesty of a great building or painting, requires effort. This outlay will be more than amply repaid by a great enrichment of the journey through this life. The second section of the Bibliography therefore suggests books for further reading which will illuminate the aesthetic experience.

The third group, more directly and narrowly related to the text, is for the guidance of those who require detailed and specialised information. It is followed by a few suggestions, all important books, of studies of related subjects.

1. THE CHURCH OF SCOTLAND

GORDON DONALDSON	'Scotland, Church and Nation through Sixteen Centuries' (*S.C.M.*)
G. F. MACLEOD	'We Shall Rebuild' (*Iona*)
W. D. MAXWELL	'An Outline of Christian Worship' (*Oxford*)
W. D. MAXWELL	'A History of Worship in the Church of Scotland' (*Oxford*)
W. D. MAXWELL	'John Knox's Genevan Service Book' (*Oliver & Boyd*)
G. W. SPROTT	'Worship and Offices in the Church of Scotland' (*Blackwood*)
CHARLES L. WARR	'The Presbyterian Tradition' (*Maclehose*)
H. J. WOTHERSPOON AND J. M. KIRKPATRICK	'A Manual of Church Doctrine According to the Church of Scotland' (Second edition revised by T. F. Torrance and R. Selby Wright) (*Oxford*)
R. SELBY WRIGHT	'The Morning Service on the Lord's Day' (*Blackwood*)
	'The Directory of the Public Worship of God agreed upon by the Assembly of Divines of Westminster' (*Blackwood and others*)

2. CHURCH BUILDINGS

A. L. DRUMMOND	'The Church Architecture of Protestantism' (*Clark*)
PETER HAMMOND	'Church Architecture and the Liturgy' (*Architectural Press*)
PETER HAMMOND	'Towards a Church Architecture' (*Architectural Press*)
GEORGE HAY	'The Architecture of Scottish Post-Reformation Churches' (*Oxford*)
IAN LINDSAY	'The Scottish Parish Kirk' (*St Andrew's Press*)
D. MACGIBBON AND I. ROSS	'The Ecclesiastical Architecture of Scotland', 3 vols. (*Douglas*) 1897
EDWARD D. MILLS	'The Modern Church' (*Architectural Press*)
E. LIDDELL ARMITAGE	'Stained Glass' (*Leonard Hill*)
H. BAGENAL	'Acoustics and Planning Against Noise' (*Methuen*)

H. BAGENAL AND A. WOOD	'Planning for Good Acoustics' (*Methuen*)
ALEC CLIFTON-TAYLOR	'The Pattern of English Building' (*Batsford*)
G. FERGUSON	'Signs and Symbols in Christian Art' (*Oxford*)
N. GRAY	'Lettering on Buildings' (*Architectural Press*)
S. HEATH	'The Romance of Symbolism' (*Griffiths*) 1909
INNES OF LEARNEY	'Scots Heraldry' (*Oliver & Boyd*)
C. AND H. LYNCH-ROBERTSON	'Intelligible Heraldry' (*Macdonald*)
P. WHITING	'Floor Finishes' (*Spon.*)

3. AESTHETICS.

BERNARD BERENSON	'Aesthetics and History' (*Constable*)
E. H. GOMBRICH	'The Story of Art' (*Phaidon*)
E. H. GOMBRICH	'Art and Illusion' (*Phaidon*)
EDGAR WIND	'Art and Anarchy' (*Faber*)

4. GENERAL

G. W. O. ADDLESHAW AND FREDERICK ETCHELLS	'The Architectural Setting for Anglican Worship' (*Faber & Faber*)
KENNETH CLARK	'The Gothic Revival. A Study in the History of Taste' (*Constable*)
J. FITCHEN	'The Construction of Gothic Cathedrals' (*Oxford*)
BANISTER FLETCHER	'A History of Architecture on the Comparative Method' (*Athlone*)
J. ARNOTT HAMILTON	'Byzantine Architecture and Decoration' (*Batsford*)
J. M. MACKINLAY	'Ancient Church Dedications in Scotland', 2 vols. (*Douglas*) 1914
NICOLAUS PEVSNER	'An Outline of European Architecture' (*Penguin*)
STEEN E. RASMUSSEN	'Experiencing Architecture' (*Chapman & Hall*)
ROBERT SENCOURT	'The Consecration of Genius' (*Hollis & Carter*)
JOHN SUMMERSON	'Heavenly Mansions' (*Cresset Press*)
R. WITTKOWER	'Architectural Principles in the Age of Humanism' (*Tiranti*)